THE SECOND RING

A JEWELER'S GUIDE TO COMPUTERS

by

S. M. HICKEL

GG,GJ

ILLUSTRATED BY BETTY PETERSON

Editors

Betty Peterson

Sue McNamara

Jean Hickel

Published by

Pimiteoui Publications
P.O. Box 48-1
Rodney, MI 49342-0048

First Printing, June 1985

92 91 90 89 88 87 86   8 7 6 5 4 3 2 1

Pimiteoui Publications
The Second Ring: A Jeweler's Guide to Computers

ISBN 0-934235-00-5

The Second Ring

Contents

FOREWARD

"In this modern age, when computer technology seems to be taking over America, it is easy for the small merchant to fall behind because the average jeweler lacks the knowledge of computers to keep up.

Nevertheless, many jewelers have tried using computers for managing inventory as well as accounting and payroll activities. But, horror stories abound because the computer salesperson knows so little about jewelry, and the jeweler so little about the computer. The jeweler who does computerize his operation learns finally how to adapt it to his own business and finds real satisfaction in having it in place, but often this could have been achieved more quickly and much more economically had all involved really been aware of how to achieve the benefits.

Mr. Hickel has addressed the question of computerization of the jewelry operation in a well organized manner. The author discusses what computers can do for a jeweler and what they can't do. He addresses the conflict between the impulse to computerize immediately and the often-encountered inclination to wait for the next generation of equipment or the next price reduction.

Essentially, "The Second Ring" helps potential computer users among jewelers to consider the pros and cons. Among the purposes it serves is to suggest the important questions one should ask oneself, and those to ask computer salespeople.

Mr. Hickel goes beyond simple computerization of bookkeeping, inventory, and payroll, also discussing telecommunications, computerizing appraisal work, the use of mailing lists, the customer data base, and other factors that can provide a new dimension for an effective businessman.

"The Second Ring: A Jeweler's Guide to Computers" is a very useful addition to the literature available to jewelers today. In my opinion, this is a needed book arriving just in time."

Richard T. Liddicoat, Jr.
2/20/85

PREFACE

In 1982, I attended the Illinois Jeweler's Association trade show. One of the seminars was about computer software for the jewelry industry. Other seminars -- on appraisals, on recutting damaged diamonds, on gemology -- were well attended, but not the computer seminar. The jewelers who did attend sat politely through the presentation, and at the end, when asked if there were any questions, few of us responded and most left promptly.

At another jewelry show the next year, among the tables of exhibitors was a computer vendor who specialized in software for the jeweler. Again I noticed the crowds at other exhibitor's tables, ie. non-oxidizing bench torches, colored stones, and more, but few of us spoke to the computer vendor.

And yet during those two years, it seemed that everywhere I went, computers were mentioned. Why, then, was their this appararent lack of interest in a computer system developed for the jeweler? Was it a lack of need for the product? Was it a terrible product? I didn't really know.

I made a decision to learn as much as possible about computers. I wanted to know what all the exitement was about, and to know what the computer could do for me -- a jeweler, appraiser, and gemologist.

Over the next two years, I studied, read, listened, and questioned. Every salesperson in every computer store in Peoria, Illinois and later in Grand Rapids, Michigan saw me at least once. As I grew in understanding, I helped start, first one computer club, and then another.

Finally, after many months of long days at work and later at home with the computer, with software, with computer books, with computer magazines, I had the answer or so I believed, as to why there was so little interest in computer software for the jeweler: the problem, I thought, was the jewelers lack of knowledge about computers. It took me two years to reach a level of understanding where I knew the right questions to ask a computer vendor; it is no wonder, then, why the jewelers who attended that seminar with me in 1982 left the room with few questions asked.

It was then that I decided to write this book. Because I saw the great potential of the computer as a tool for the jeweler, I believed this book would be of some small benefit to the jewelry industry.

In short, this book is the culmination of what I have learned; a summary of what I believe worthwhile for the jeweler to know about computers. If it saves you any time, or gives you an idea that makes you money, or gives you an understanding of computers that you would not otherwise have, the book will have succeeded.

- SMH -

Acknowledgement

To Jean, Betty & Roger, Mom & Dad, Lawson, Mike,
Matt, Sue, and Grandma.

thanks

Notes to the Reader:

Computer terminology can be complex, to say the least. In order to make your reading easier, I have begun most chapters with a mini-glossary that provides definitions of the unfamiliar terms I've used within that section. This has been done to avoid having those of you who are familiar with computers having to stumble over long, drawn-out definitions in the text at every turn, and to give the reader less experienced in the world of computers a quick reference when we arrive at those chapters containing more technical information.

The pronoun "he" has been used throughout this text to refer to individuals of both sexes. This was done merely for simplicity and ease of writing; it should not be considered a reflection on gender, but should serve as reference to members of humankind in general.

THE SECOND RING

"In the ancient times before men were counted amongst the animals, God asked the trees, 'If I create Man, what would be the bravest thing he would do?' The ancient oak replied, 'He would make mighty ships of the strongest trees and sail upon your seas.' The tall pines said, 'He would carve bows from the sinewest of trees to hunt the wild beasts.' Each tree replied until all were heard. Still, God had not heard anything that pleased him."

"Suddenly, the lowest form of life in the forest spoke. It was the mushroom. 'Forgive me mighty one for speaking. I have heard each tree speak; and they say nothing because they speak of what would glorify themselves. Behold, I am the least of your creations; I can only speak from my own dreams. Should you create Man, he will know the first ring as I do. This first ring will be the ring of his friends, family, and neighbors. It, like you, has neither a beginning nor an end. While his ring may grow, as mine does, to encompass much, it will both limit and support him. His horizons will be finite, his ambitions limited, his hopes encircled. I proclaim, the bravest thing that Man could do would be to reach beyond this first ring and create a second, the second ring. Like a drop of dew falling upon the still surface of a lake, the second ring would beget a third and a third a fourth even unto infinity. For it is with the second ring that Man would become like you, with neither a beginning nor an end, and touch the infinite.'"

"Upon hearing this, God was pleased. 'I shall make him in my own image and likeness, and I shall place you, the lowliest of my creations, in all the places where Man shall walk so that he might see the first ring. I shall place wonder in his heart. With this wonder Man shall come to know that he can reach beyond the first ring.'"

-an old Gaelic legend-

INTRODUCTION

The computer. It can strike fear in the heart of the most successful entrepreneur. It can bring to mind such unfamiliar terms as microprocessor, software, modems and random-access-memory. And, it can be a major source of frustration if your competition becomes "computerized" before you do.

In recent years, more and more jewelers have begun to recognize the value of computers. From appraisals to accounts receivable, from general ledger to inventory control, the computer is making its presence known in the jewelry industry.

And, it's giving those jewelers who use the computer, a competitive edge. This book will show you why.

While computer technology has grown by leaps and bounds in recent years, the cost of owning a computer hasn't. For less than $6000, today's jeweler can purchase a computer which far surpasses the capability of those costing many times as much only years ago. And, the host of computer software now available can save hours of work through the automation of countless tasks.

The jewelry industry today is a competitive one. Not only must we as jewelers compete with one another for our share of discretionary income, but we must also share that dollar with discount houses, stereo and video stores, new car dealers and more.

It is becoming increasingly important for the jeweler to establish -- and maintain -- a competitive edge. One way to do so is to streamline our businesses so that every sale results in the greatest contribution to the bottom line -- profit. The computer can be your key to this kind of success. And, it can open the door to making your staff far more productive than otherwise thought possible.

Now that the price of computers (microprocessors) has

tumbled to within the grasp of nearly all of private enterprise, many small-business owners and managers are beginning to look into the use of computers. This book is a window through which you can see them more clearly.

You will learn simple computer jargon, and become familiar with the many, more technical uses of the computer. You will come to understand the important developments in the computer field, and the effect of those advances on computer owners and users in the future.

You will read about present and future computer related jewelry applications and potential uses, and gain first-hand knowledge in how the two fields relate to one another. And, you'll learn how computers evolved and where current trends may lead.

Most importantly, you'll be exposed to the world of computers in a comprehensive, concise manner. Any you'll be given guidelines upon which to base your decisions about whether, how, and when to use a computer of your own.

Part I talks about computers in general terms, and gives you an idea of what -- and how much -- to expect from them.

Part II discusses the Ideal Jewelry Program (I.J.P.) -- a program which will one day give the jeweler the means to fully computerize his operations, and leave his business running like a fine-tuned, well-oiled machine. Many of the individual programs in the I.J.P. are available to you today. And, while not package specifically for jewelers, most of them can be fairly easily adapted to meet your business needs. Others are still in the making -- yet, knowing about them will give you an edge when they his the market in the near future.

In Part III, you'll learn more about the history, current trends and communicative nature of computers. This will give you the information necessary to make sound decisions on what computers and software programs are best for you and from which companies to purchase them.

Finally, Part IV deals with future trends in computer software and hardware developments, and what they mean to you as a user. And, more specifically, you will be given a birds-eye view of the future of the jewelry industry and the role computers will play within it.

This book was not written for the computer wizard -- although I'd like to think that that person could still learn something from what it contains. Rather, it was written for the jeweler with one store on Mainstreet, Downtown, U.S.A. and for his colleague with a chain of 500 jewelry store outlets across the nation. Each of them share the desire to know more about how a computer could affect his productivity and profitability in the years ahead.

Just as jewelry appraisers should study gemology to best do their jobs, so can the jeweler gain a better grasp of computers by studying them. A multitude of how-to computer books are available that can help you obtain the maximum benefit from a computer. But, reading all of that material could take years. This book provides you with one reference source that give you a background from which to expand. And, it is tailored specifically to the use of computers in the jewelry industry -- your industry.

If you own or plan to buy a computer -- or if you're merely curious about how computers can help make your business tick -- this book was written with you in mind.

Welcome to the world of computers!

ABOUT THE AUTHOR

Steve Hickel has worked as an appraiser and gemologist since 1981. Before this he worked himself up through the ranks in the United States Navy, from a Seaman Recruit through Lieutenant. In 1981, he was awarded the Navy Commendation Medal while serving as the Transportation Officer at the Philadelphia Naval Shipyard. He served on two nuclear submarines and is trained in the Navy's "business" officer ranks: the Supply Corps. Here he received extensive experience in inventory control and management skills -- skills that find a welcome place in the jewelry business.

Steve holds a Bachelor's Degree in psychology from Duquesne University. He is widely travelled and can speak both French and German fluently.

Steve is a Graduate Jeweler of the Canandian Jewellery Institute, Toronto, Canada and an Affiliate of the American Gem Society. In addition, Steve holds the title of Graduate Gemologist with his diploma dated October, 1981.

Computers became a hobby and later a part-time profession for Steve while working as a Gemologist. He has been a consultant for a major manufacturing firm; he helped develop a series of kinematic programs for a common household product. Further, he first co-founded the Peoria, Illinois User Group for IBM Personal Computers and compatibles, and later he co-founded the Grand Rapids, Michigan User Group for which he is currently serving as President.

Steve has been involved in the Kiwanis club and is an active Naval Reservist; he is currently the Commanding Officer for a Naval Reserve Supply Detachment.

– PART 1 –

WHAT COMPUTERS CAN DO FOR YOU

1

A DIAMOND IN THE ROUGH

DISCUSSION OF TERMS

DATA--This term denotes all information (ie. facts, figures, symbols) that can be stored on, used by, and computed with a computer.

DATA BASE--An extensive file of information on a particular topic that is continually updated.

TELECOMMUNICATE--A means of transferring data through electrical means, ie. telephone and radio. Computers are capable of transfering vast quantities of information through telecommunications.

It's been said that a diamond is a woman's best friend. History may show that, for the modern jeweler, the computer holds that honor. No tool ever created has managed to expand so thoroughly the minds and lives of so many. And, each year, more and more businesspeople are turning to the computer to reach new horizons in sales and service.

There is little doubt that the 1980's and 1990's will be boom years for service-oriented businesses. Because the jewelry business has been built largely upon service and reputation, the computer can help you to reach an even higher level of service to the consumer.

In this sense, the computer is still a diamond-in-the-rough. Yet, each year, more and more jewelers discover its hidden beauty. And, constant improvements in technology continue to chip away at its limitations, revealing an increasingly brilliant new method of business management.

Obviously, the computer's greatest strength lies in its ability to process large amounts of data. During the next 20 years, the computer will not only show you who your market is, but will help you to capture a greater slice of it; to break ground in new markets; and to acquire the means to accomplish all these things and more.

If we as jewelers hope to channel the flow of jewelry purchases from mass merchandisers back to the jewelry store, we must reach out to the jewelry-buying public with this message: "For every occasion, the jewelry store is the best place to buy jewelry."

To accomplish this, we'll need a tool no less powerful than the computer. For, with it, we'll have access to the kind and quantity of information that can make this hope a reality.

In short, the computer can help us reach beyond our "first ring." When used to automate bookkeeping chores such as word processing, inventory control, accounts receivable, payroll, mailing list preparation, general ledger, accounts payable, and others, the computer can save you a significant amount of time and money.

Such automation can reduce outside accounting services, lessen the bookkeeping work load and increase the productivity of your staff.

The computer does this first by giving you a means to collect data for a large Customer Data Base. This "base" is a compilation of information about those people who shop at your store. It's information that can help you more fully understand your customers in general. Then, through an analysis of your customer data base, you can get a more specific profile of your typical customer -- the one to which you can and should direct more of your selling efforts. And, this data can, in turn, help you pinpoint geographic areas in which you are less succesful -- those that demand your marketing attention.

In addition, by using the computer to prepare appraisals, to perform three-dimensional diamond sales

A COMPUTER, WHEN GIVEN USEFUL INFORMATION, PRODUCES USEFUL INFORMATION

Figure 1.1.1

presentations and customer education programs, to telecommunicate to a new, expanding electronic marketplace, and to access information enabling you to manage your time, money and people better, you can increase your ability to compete in the market place. Table 1.1.1 provides a partial summary of the tasks made easier by the computer.

Word Processing	Spreadsheet
Mailing List	Education
Inventory Control	Accounts Payable
Accounts Receivable	General Ledger
Payroll	Customer Data Profile
Telecommunications	Computer Aided Design
Computer Aided Manufacturing	Electronic Mail
Diamond Sales (3-D Demo)	Leisure
Cash Flow Analysis	Sales Reports
Training	Profiles of Customers
Marketing Analysis	Appraisals
Gemological Expert System	

TASKS MADE EASIER BY AUTOMATION

Table 1.1.1

You might say that in a store whose volume is less than $1,000,000 per year, that some of these tasks would be better done manually. But, with present computers and the sophistication and ease of use of new software, these things can be done both quicker and easier. Once you see the potential in solving these previously hand-done chores by computer, you'll be hooked.

Let's pause to look at an example of how these tasks work into a total computerized program for you.

We'll begin by inputting the customer addresses on your daily receipts into the computer. The computer can then give you a fast report on the geographic locations of customers that most and least frequently shop in your store (you can request a breakdown by zip code). The logical next step would be to then concentrate advertising dollars into both of these locations -- to totally develop the potential of these areas, too. That's just one of many examples of how the computer can provide you with useful information in a fraction of the time it would take for you to come up with those results manually.

Finally, when used as a word processor, the computer can produce correspondence and appraisals, giving a professional appearance to your store's documents, and thus enhancing its image.

If you find yourself lagging behind the competition because they get better and more useful market data from a computer -- or if you simply find that your manual recordkeeping methods are too time-consuming -- a computer can help. The remainder of this book is designed to bring you to a better level of understanding about computers -- one that will allow you to reap tremendous benefits by bringing this diamond of modern technology out of the "rough."

2

MAN
OF
THE YEAR

DISCUSSION OF TERMS

AUTOMATION--The general practice of applying computers to solve or assist with administrative, sales, accounting, and other general business matters. Automation may be implemented in whole or part through the use of computers in a daily business atmosphere.

DISKS--Magnetic storage devices that hold or store a program by magnetic pulses. Programs are loaded into random read-write memory (RAM) from disk. Disks can be floppy, hard, or laser. Each has its own unique characteristics and advantages. The most common disk on microcomputers is floppy disks; whereas, owing to their greater storage capacity, disks supermicro-, mini- and mainframe computers are usually hard disks (far greater storage capacity). With new advances in laser technology, laser disks capable of billions of characters of storage are finding their way into computer storage devices, but as yet these devices can not be easily written to and usually only once. This makes them a good archival (for future reference only) storage device, yet limits them from day to day usage.

LASER--A coherent beam of light, emitted from a device designed to create light energy at one frequency. LASER stands for Light Amplification by Stimulation of Emission of Radiation. The Jewelry industry currently uses lasers for the finger printing of transparent gemstones, ie. GEMPRINT. Soon disk storage devices will be available to the jeweler that will store billions of pieces of information or the equivalent of over 250,000 double spaced pages (more than an encyclopedia).

MAINFRAME--Large computers that process quantities of data at rapid speeds with access to billions of characters of data. They are characterized by their multi-user and multi-tasking nature.

MICROCOMPUTER--A small computer system consisting basically of a monitor screen, keyboard and limited data storage. It is based upon a microprocessor. It is versatile due to small size, trustworthy performance and low weight, power, and cost. As the ability of those using microcomputers increases, as the number of those using microcomputers increases, and as the technology to create more powerful microprocessors continues, the microcomputer will soon outstrip its older, but bigger cousins -- the mini- and the mainframe computer. This new micro, used by the super users of the next decade will be called a supermicrocomputer.

MICROPROCESSORS--The small single silicon chip on which is contained the electronic components of an entire central processor. It is one of the main parts of a microcomputer. This is the brain of the computer in which all the computations are performed in binary form. A microprocessor can be compared to thousands of tiny on-off switches or gates. These switches perform the logic for which computers are so noted. Most are the size of wafer cookies or smaller.

MINICOMPUTER--A computer system having greater performance capabilities and higher prices than microcomputers, but with less storage, slower processing speeds, and lowei cost than a mainframe computer. The concept of minicomputer is soon to merge with the concept of the supermicrocomputer. In general, minicomputers offer what microcomputers offer, but more. Many minicomputers, however, do not share compatibility with their junior cousins--the microcomputer. For this reason, the minicomputer is often used in turnkey systems, which is a vertical application for a specific industry. In other words, on minicomputers there is less variety of software available than on microcomputers, but what minicomputers do offer over the microcomputer is usually more powerful software that is designed to do one or more related tasks extemely well. More and more minicomputers are turning to a generic operating system, such as UNIX, so that the general applications that are available for the many different brands of minicomputers can be used on most minicomputers (this saves on redevelopment costs).

MULTI-TASKING--More than one program is run on a computer at the same time. One program runs in the foreground and others in background. Some computers, through the use of windows, can run more than one application in the foreground.

MULTI-USER--More than one terminal can be used at the same time to run more than one program.

RANDOM (READ-WRITE) ACCESS MEMORY (RAM)--a very fast method of retrieving information at any storage location in the memory. This is the location to where programs are loaded to and the medium in which they operate to carry out their assigned functions (think of it as an electronic warehouse in which data--electronic on-off signals--are constantly being shipped, stored, and moved).

SUPERMICROCOMPUTER--The melding of the microcomputer with the minicomputer in a low cost, high power unit, containing many of the features of both, and usually at a lower cost than a minicomputer (it could also be called a very powerful microcomputer).

In 1982, the editors of Time Magazine bestowed upon the computer their coveted "Man of the Year" distinction. That year, computer vendors sold more computers than ever before . . . and some of those buyers were undoubtedly jewelers.

Yet, if you're considering hiring this "Man of the Year," a word of caution is in order. Don't buy a computer with the hope of solving all your business problems until you consider this: To make the most of a computer will take you from six months to two years. And, during this time, your computer will probably be under-utilized.

The reasons for this vary. Experts attribute it to the initial learning curve associated with understanding the various capabilities and functions of the computer. But, whatever the reason, for you and your employees to learn to use a computer successfully, you must be prepared to devote a great deal of time to making its use profitable.

Put simply, computers take time. The computer industry does strive faithfully to reduce the learning curve for first-time computer users. Some call this concept user-friendliness -- an effort to make computers more "friendly", more simple, to work with. Yet, even though computers have and continue to become more user-friendly, a jeweler considering the automation of his store(s) must have a very clear grasp of his business and its organization. A computer will not organize it for him. It can only make tasks occurring within an established organizational structure more simple.

Far too many businesspeople believe that, by simply computerizing their businesses, they can save time and money. Not so. The need to clearly define your business has never been greater. And, if you want a computer to work for you, your business must work, too. If it doesn't, computerization may only make matters worse.

Also, many business owners fall prey to another misconception. Computers do not necessarily ease the burden of maintaining a trained staff by replacing one or more employees altogether. Rather, the computer will make more demands on your business, your people and you -- an important fact to consider.

The computer can generate two kinds of data: useful and useless. In order to provide consistently beneficial information, it requires data discipline. In essence, this means that, to retrieve useful data from a computer, information must be carefully structured and maintained within the computer's memory (This memory is called Random Read-Write Access Memory (RAM), and is an integral part of computer operations), and within the magnetic disks that are used to store the data when the computer is not using it

COMPUTERS CAN HELP; NOT TAKE OVER

Figure 1.2.1

Thus, you may find that you will have to first systematize your business in a manner that will enable a smooth transition from manual to automated procedures. Interestingly, those tasks which remain manual after such automation often become easier themselves as a result of it.

By forcing you to organize (or reorganize) your business, computerization brings you face to face with the strengths and weaknesses of your operations. As a result, you will find yourself making decisions that will guide your business more smoothly for years to come. Thus, as competition for the jewelry dollar increases, through automation, you will be better able to keep your finger on the pulse of your business.

Because you must, at least in part, change some of your present procedures to best make use of the computer's capabilities, installation of a computer in a jewelry store is hard work. It requires hours of management time -- valuable time that could be spent on other chores.

At this point, take just a moment to think about the man-hours it now takes to do the tasks you will be automating. Table 1.2.2 can help you determine your distribution of labor. Those hours can then be tallied to provide a current estimate of labor and time.

Next, you can look at this information and see how much time can be saved by implementing a computer. In general, the more repetitive and frequent the task, the more suitable it is for automation.

An example of this is payroll -- a task that is usually done frequently and in repetition. If you have only three or four people on staff, then the time and expense necessary to automate payroll is negated. If, on the other hand, you have ten or more people on the payroll, you may want to strongly consider automating this function. But, in doing so, you might find yourself needing to make changes. For instance, if you payroll is on a weekly schedule, you may find you have to consider moving the pay period to a two-week or monthly cycle in order to free up additional hours for you bookkeepers to devote extra time to learning computer operations.

In addition to adding up the man-hours for each task that is considered for automation, you should also put on paper a five-year or at least a one-year business plan, asking yourself, "Where do I want my store(s) to be in five years?"

By setting long-term goals, you can see more clearly where the computer will best fit into your business, how large a system you will need, and how long it could be used before you outgrow it.

These goals should remain flexible: the plan should not be too general nor too specific. It is merely intended to show you how the computer will save you time and money, or whether it will be an extra, unneeded expense.

Naturally expense is a major consideration in purchasing a computer. Later in this book, we will be discussing computers and software (the languages, programs, and processes of a computer system). Over 32,000 ready-to-run software packages, available in about 90,000 versions and capable of running on computers of all sizes can be purchased. The cost for these software programs runs from anywhere between free to over $100,000 dollars. Generally, the average jeweler will need either a microcomputer or minicomputer. Both of these types of computers sell for less than $20,000, and the prices veer downward every month.

To my knowledge, the least expensive jewelry-related software program in existence costs $795. When you add the cost of a computer to that, you'll find you must now spend a minimum of $3,800 to automate parts of your business.

Except for the most demanding situations, a one store operation can use a microcomputer to automate. Multi-store operations will almost always require a minicomputer or a supermicrocomputer. The basic differences between the two are shown in Table 1.2.1

MICROCOMPUTER	MINICOMPUTER (supermicrocomputer)
Under $6000.00	Over $6000.00
16k to 640k RAM	128k To Over 2M RAM
Floppy Or Hard Disk (To 20MB)	Usually Hard Disk (To Over 200MB)
Usually single-user	Usually multi-user
Usually single-tasking	Usually multi-tasking
More software Available	Less Available
Cheaper software	More Expensive
Software More Generic	Software Tied To Comp.
Slower Processors	Faster Processors

COMPARES MICROCOMPUTER TO MINICOMPUTER

Table 1.2.1

In general, then, a properly used computer can release you from the burden of spending too much time on menial or tedious jobs. In some cases, although not saving time, the computer can provide for greater productivity in the same amount of time. In other cases, it may even take longer to complete a job.

In order to see clearly those areas where a computer may be of greatest benefit to you, take the time to fill out the forms provided in tables 1.2.2 and 1.2.3 (Appendix A has blank samples of these forms).

Number of employees currently employed?____5_________
List all employee job titles and hours each works per week:

Titles	Hours per week
(example)_OWNER______	_50__
(example)_MANAGER____	_60__
____________________	_.___
____________________	_.___
____________________	_.___
____________________	_.___
____________________	_.___
____________________	_.___
____________________	_.___
____________________	_.___
	TOTAL HRS_260_

APPROXIMATE TOTAL HOURS OF ALL EMPLOYEES

Table 1.2.2

List by job title hours performed in the below (per week):

Job title_(example)__Manager____	HOURS
Sales presentations to customers	_15__
Housekeeping and cleaning	_____
Store meetings	_1___
Training(on the job)	_3___
Windows and displays	_____
Appraisals	_3___
Putting out inventory	_____
Advertising	_2___
Repair and appraisal take in	_1___
Repair work	_____
Bookkeeping	
a. Accounts payable	_____
b. Accounts receivable	_____
c. Payroll	_____
d. Word processing and typing	_____
e. Open-to-buys	_2___
f. Financial analysis and budgeting	_2___
g. Repair job tracking	.5___
h. Inventory control	_1___
i. General Ledger	_____
j. Mailing lists	_1___
k. File upkeep	_____
l. General record maintenance	_____
m. Receiving stock	_____
n. Transferring stock	_____
o. Shipping stock	_____
p. Layaway tracking	_____
q. Other	_____
Management	
a. Financial planning	_1___
b. Hiring	_1___
c. Memo and reports	_2___
d. Follow-up	_1___
e. Troubleshooting	_2___
f. Training	_1___
g. Scheduling	_3___
h. Entertaining	_2___
i. Lectures and meetings	_3___
j. Salesman and buying	_3___
k. Work brought home	_3___
l. Scheduling	_2___
TOTAL HOURS	_60__

BREAKDOWN BY JOB OF HOURS WORKED

Table 1.2.3

In summary, you should determine -- if possible, before purchasing a computer -- what it is you wish to automate. Further, you must be organized so that the computer will compliment your store's operations, not hinder them.

You should know where you want to be in five years in order to effectively guide your organization. and, lastly, you must budget for a computer. After deciding to automate and after shopping for the software and the specific computer that will be required to accomplish your objectives, you should have a very good idea of how much you'll need to spend.

Whether you've purchased a computer already, or are still in the planning stages, please keep this in mind: computers do not have all the answers; they are tools that demand good management -- they cannot do the managing for you.

A TOOL FOR PROFITABILITY

Figure 1.2.2

In future years, when computers become powerful enough to model human thinking, they will be able to offer us advice. Today, however, we are still on our own. Your resolve to automate, or to wait to do so, will in large part be determined by your desire to remain competitive. When used correctly, the computer will give you that extra leverage for which you may be searching. It's leverage that is virtually imperative. For, as more and more businesses turn to computers, and more and more employees learn to use them effectively, the honed edge of competition will become ever sharper.

3

TO BUY OR NOT TO BUY

DISCUSSION OF TERMS

BITS--Binary digit-abbreviated. Meaning one of two values ((on-off) (1-0) (yes/no) (high voltage/low voltage)). The bit is like a 2 letter alphabet. With this alphabet, the computer can perform Binary arithmetic. George Boole and Leibnitz were among the first to discover the capabilities of a thinking machine using bits to perform calculations. The computer merely extends the power of the pen to perform logical binary computations.

BYTE--Means eight bits used as a unit, it can be two numbers or one character. A byte can be regarded as a word made up of the alphabet of bits. The more bytes the machine is capable of moving around within its processor at the same time, the larger is its short term memory and ability to process quickly. That is why an 8 bit machine is slower than a 16 bit machine is slower than a 32 bit machine. In fact, an 8 bit machine can address as much as 2 to the 8th memory locations; a 16 bit machine as much as 2 to the 16th memory locations; and a 32 bit machine as much as 2 to the 32nd memory locations. Programs that are written for a 32 bit machine can be larger and will run faster than, let's say, a 16 bit machine.

WHAT-IF--An analysis of financial data using an electronic spreadsheet. The analysis is sped up owing to the ability of the computer and the spreadsheet program to quickly change key figures and numbers that permits the fast recalculation of results. By properly using modern electronic spreadsheet programs, the Jeweler can develop and change a dynamic model of his business just by pressing a few keystrokes of a keyboard. This ability to see these changes developed within seconds of each other often lets the jeweler make extremely important management decisions that otherwise could not have been made.

PERIPHERALS--In regard to computers, these are the accessory equipment that gives the computer its various abilities to communicate with the humankind, ie. printers, keyboards, monitors, and so forth. Another term commonly used is Input/Output (I/O) devices.

PROGRAM--This is the instructions that are saved on disk, loaded into Random Read-Write Memory (RAM) when needed, and run on a microprocessor to carry out the programmers designed function. A program can be very simple or very complex. The program is what makes the machine behave for the user in the manner that he desires. Even the fastest most sophisticated computer is useless unless it also has fast and sophisticated programs written for it. Consider that it is not only the computer but the software that will make you and your business both more productive and more profitable. It is true that minicomputer programs are often more sophisticated than those of microcomputer programs but are limited in the range of available applications. Here is where the microcomputer shines -- in the breadth of programs available for it. As more and more programs are written for microcomputers and as their computing power increases, the the distinction between microcomputers and minicomputers will blur thus the word, "supermicrocomputer."

Never has the computer been more widely available for so little money. For example, the Apple "MacIntosh" computer -- the state-of-the-art microcomputer on the personal computer market today, costs about $2,500. The IBM Personal Computer (IBM PC) is available for nearly the same price. In short, computers have never been more affordable, nor has the market for them ever had such great potential.

In 1979, when the Apple computer and Visicalc -- the original microcomputer spreadsheet program -- met for the first time, high-powered financial analysis tools landed on the desk of small businessmen. Since then, over 6,100 programs have been written for the IBM PC, more than 6,400 for the Apple II and IIE, and in excess of 5,000 for the TRS-80 Model series of Tandy (Radio Shack) computers.

Please note that the programs make the machine a tool. The better the programs that are written for a machine, the more versatile, useful, and powerful the computer will be. To give you an idea of the versatility of programs available of microcomputers today, please look at Figure 1.3.1. It shows the ratio of major application programs written for just one microcomputer on the market today -- the IBM Personal Computer (PC).

With the arrival of the IBM PC, computers went from the 8-bit standard (remember -- bits are the most basic on-off signal of the electronic computer. The more bits, the faster the computer can process data) to the more powerful 16-bit standard -- a move that significantly enhanced the potential of programs written for these microcomputers. Companies now market programs that vie the power of minicomputers and mainframe computers of just a few years ago.

Further with the arrival of the "MacIntosh" series of computers by Apple Computer Corporation of Cupertino, California, the microcomputer has been vaulted into the world of 32 bits (a very fast microprocessor previously seen only on much more expensive computers). The power and versatility of these computers are extraordinary.

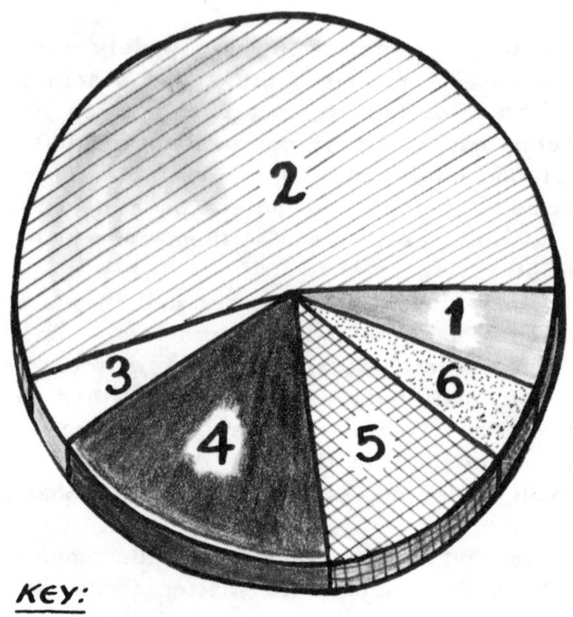

THE RATIO OF SOFTWARE AVAILABLE FOR IBM PC

Figure 1.3.1

Almost all jewelers would find that a minicomputer or a microcomputer will fill almost all their computing needs.

Since the price of today's newest computers will fall tomorrow (it is interesting to note that the newest equipment seems to fill the old equipment's incumbent price levels), why shouldn't you wait to buy? Many businesspeople say, "Oh, if I buy now there will probably be a drastic change in computers; prices will be slashed and I will be stuck with an antiquated machine."

It is true: changes are occurring every day. The crucial question to which you should address yourself is this: "If I buy a computer now will it serve its purpose?"

The answer to that question is often a resounding, "Yes!" For many applications, the computer can be an invaluable aid to you right now -- today. You can discover that, with electronic spreadsheets and the aid of your accountant, you'll be able to establish a financial model of your business. By playing "What-if" analysis, you can see changes in that model just by changing key elements of it in the computer.

For example, what if sales were to drop by 15%? What effect would that have on your business's profit? In this regard, you can discover the computer to be a valuable business partner.

But, what if you wait? What will you gain?

The price plateau for the state-of-the-art computer will probably not drop dramatically over the next few years; the raw computing power of these computers and their peripherals (added equipment) will increase, however, while the price for each new computer will remain fairly constant. Once a specific computer model is introduced to the market, its price tends to drop in the few years following its release. When a new model is brought to market, which improves on the old one, the introductory price seems to return to the level that the old model first occupied. Thus, by waiting, you'll eventually get more computer for your dollar.

Yet, let me share with you a little analogy before we go any farther that may serve to illustrate a point. I have an acquaintance who refuses to go to the theater. He insists that it's a waste of money. After all, every one knows that the movie showing at the theater today will be available on video cassette in a few months any way. And he doesn't have to put up with lines and he can watch it at his convenience instead of at scheduled times. Yet, so many of us still go to the theater each week. Why? Because we want to see the picture now. We want the enjoyment of watching it while it's new and fresh -- before we overhear the plot from fellow workers or the guy in the seat behind us on the airplane. Sure, we could wait. Yet, for whatever reason, it's worth it to us to spend that $3 to $5 today. Besides, who knows? In two or three years, the theater might have closed down. The picture might not be in circulation. We might have missed it altogether. Yet, my acquaintance still insists it's best -- most frugal and intelligent -- to wait.

So, by waiting to make the capital investment in a computer, you'll be able to get a state-of-the-art model.

You will, however, be sacrificing the one advantage created by acquiring a computer now. Another leap forward

COMPUTER AGE

Figure 1.3.2

toward the competitive edge.

Still, if you don't have the capital to invest now, waiting may be a necessity rather than a choice.

Ultimately, you're the best one to make the decision for your business. But keep this in mind. In the future, virtually every businessperson will be required to know how to use computers. They will be a business necessity. So, by implementing a computer in your business today, however slowly, you would simply have a head start on that future. And, if you haven't already, you will learn the potential of the computer as a marketing tool and more. You'll be ahead of the fastest-moving game in town.

4

RUSH HOUR AT THE COMPUTER

DISCUSSION OF TERMS

FILE--An accumulation of data on a certain topic or for a certain purpose. These are the equivalent to files in a file cabinet in that each contains information on a specific topic. Files are identified by file names.

HARDWARE--The solid, metal or "hard" component parts of a computer.

ICONS--Illustrative images used to instruct the computer to perform a particular task. The icon is similar to verbal menus but lets common symbols take the place of words. This saves space and lets more people understand choices quicker.

MODEM--A modulator-demodulator device that converts digital signals into telephone signals and back again.

ON-LINE--Denotes currently in use or over a telecommunications network, ie. He is on-line with his other store or the on-line data base contains information that I can give you as soon as I have received it.

OPERATING SYSTEM--A low level language program, usually written in assembly language, that carries out the commands of the programs in progress. It acts as the air traffic controller for software and hardware.

PROCESSING TIME--The time a computer uses to carry out the computations of a program. A computer generally does not use its processor to process but a fraction of the time. By switching back and forth between programs, a multi-tasking and multi-user computer makes use of this feature to process more than one program at nearly the same time -- to the operator is seems to be at the same time. The more bits the computer has, the quicker the computer, the more users it can have, and the more programs it can have sharing the processor. This is why some systems get bogged down when many operators vie simultaneously for processing time.

SINGLE-TASKING--One program at time can be run on the computer.

SINGLE-USER--Only one person can use a computer at a time.

TUTORIAL--A help file associated with a computer program that can usually be called upon for assistance or used to teach the operator about functions or feature of the program in use.

In the coming years, computers will be much more powerful than they are today. Table 1.4.1 will show you what you may expect in the evolution of microcomputers.

Greater Raw Processing Power
Processing Speed
More Sophisticated Programs
Cheaper Programs
Integrated Programs
Artificial Intelligence
Multi-tasking
Multi-user
Higher Resolution and Greater Use Of Graphics
Better Prices
Wider Dissemination Of Computers Throughout
Computer Networking
Greater Standardization

The Computer Evolution

Table 1.4.1

The meaning of these changes may not be self-evident. Yet, they could certainly have a profound effect on the use of computers in the jewelry business.

All business will become more and more computerized. Decisions will be based on computer-generated information of a nature that is not yet even available today. Programmers will develop software that will not only help to make decisions, but will all but make the decisions for us. The power to do this is on the horizon.

Almost all personal computers today are single-user and single-tasking. What do these terms mean? In short, single-tasking means that only one program at a time can be run on the computer. Multi-tasking means the opposite: more than one operation can be performed on the same computer at the same time. In other words, let's compare a single railroad track with the many tracks in a railroad yard. On the single railroad track only one train can move at a time, at least until it moves to a siding for another train to pass. In the railroad yard, however, many trains can move about at the same time without crashing into each other. This is the principle behind multi-tasking.

Most computers that are multi-tasking and multi-user are called minicomputers (as you may recall, though, this distinction is quickly disappearing. Table 1.2.1 compares minicomputers and microcomputers). For a computer to be multi-tasking and multi-user, it must have a central processor fast enough to handle all the flowing electrons carrying on the simultaneous tasks. Now, the average personal computer is not multi-user or multi-tasking. If two people want to use a single-user computer at the same time the one must wait for the other to finish.

In few jewelry companies is the rivalry to use installed computers a problem. Many companies may find that, in the first year of computerization, it can be a chore to keep the computer in use at all times. However, as more and more jewelers begin to use computers as executive workstations, sales tools, and as an appraisal tool and gemologist's workbench (see Ideal Jewelry Program in Part II), the computer will begin to be used for a greater part of the work day.

As computers find homes in the everyday business environment, more and more jewelry people will learn to depend on computers to earn their keep. For example, appraisers are just now beginning to use computers to assist them with their appraisals; some are even using large, on-line data bases (computer to computer communications via a modem--a device that converts computer signals into telephone language and back) from which to derive their prices, gemological information, and advice, if needed.

With so many on your staff using computers, more than one computer or terminal will eventually become necessary. This won't happen on a large scale, however, until the price of the computer drops still further or the capabilities at current prices improve.

As schools and homes absorb computers, more and more

children, students, and young adults will enter the job environment knowing, needing, and using computers. As young jewelers find a shortage of computers in the work environment, they may even bring their own computers into the workspace until you are persuaded, through sheer demand, to have one, two, or more computers.

Further, as you learn to appreciate the power of the computer as an electronic workstation, you, yourself, may find the line at the computer too long: behind your appraisers, bookkeepers, and managers.

Summary

Will this bustle to the computer take place overnight? No, probably not. The learning curve associated with the use of computers is a high hurdle. However, the advances in the computer business to make computers more friendly to the novice are intense; the computer manufacturers are taking advantage of the healthy processing powers of the newer microcomputer and minicomputers to make them user-friendly: they are installing tutorials within programs, such as on the IBM System 36 minicomputer. The operating systems of Apple's LISA and "MacIntosh" computers routinely use illustrative images called icons (such as a garbage can, meaning to erase a file). Even the IBM family of computers is moving towards icons (programs such as Vision, DESQ, and Microsoft's Windows, which run on the IBM PC, make use of icons). Both icons and tutorials devour computer memory (RAM), disk space, and processing time.

As the price of microprocessor chips, memory (RAM), and disk storage drop, the friendliness of computers increase. Further, as more and more jewelers and their employees buy computers to use at home for games and education, more and more people will understand computers, making the transition from the home computer to the business computer faster and easier than ever before.

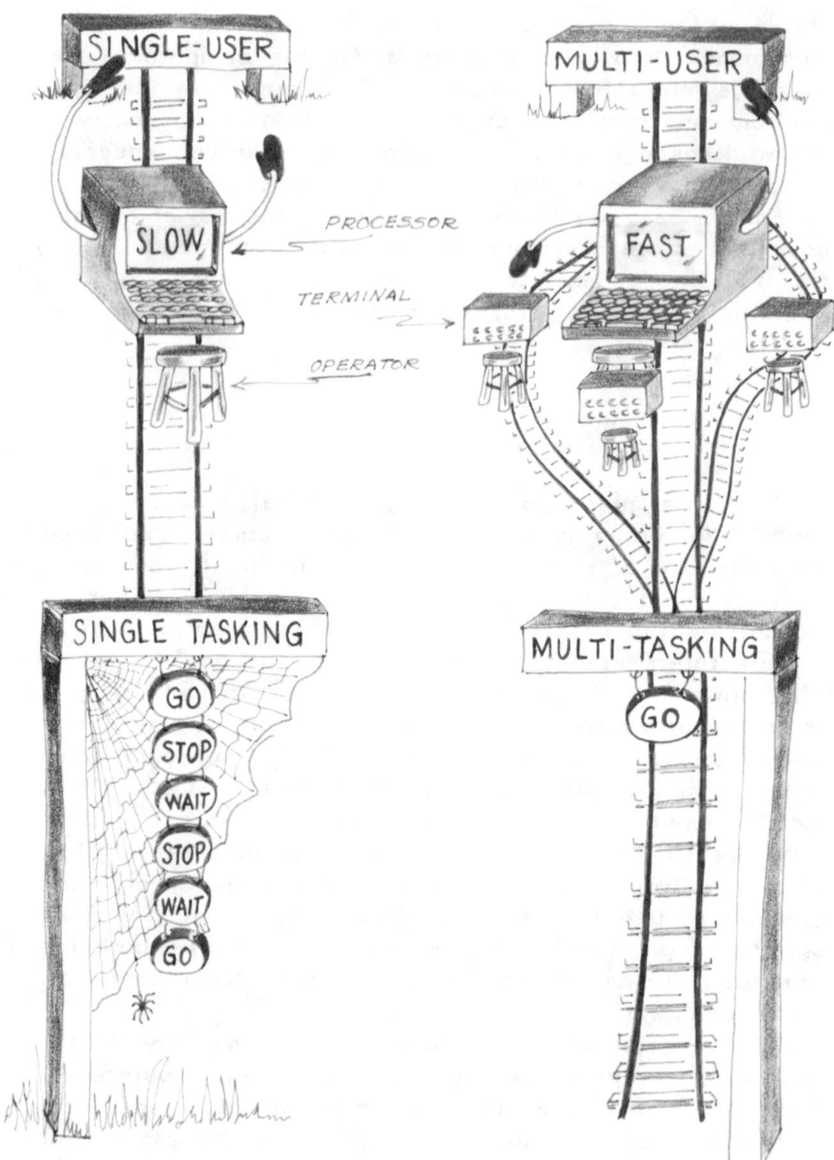

SINGLE-TASKING VERSUS MULTI-TASKING

Figure 1.4.1

AS THE POWER OF COMPUTERS GROWS...
SO DOES THEIR USER-FRIENDLINESS

Figure 1.4.2

5

GETTING WITH THE PROGRAM

DISCUSSION OF TERMS

COMMAND DRIVEN--No menus are offered to the user (although the commands could be used to create menus). The instructions or choices must be known by the user to perform various functions in a program. It offers greater flexibility and control of data.

LANGUAGE(COMPUTER)--A set of symbols a computer will understand and the rules to control those symbols. Like an infant the computer comes into the world preprogrammed with basic tools needed to perform very rudimentary functions. These processes are "burned" into the design of the computer chip and allow the computer to do housekeeping chores, ie. math and logic control and language interpreters. It is this inbred ability of the computer to understand symbols that tells the computer how to behave. Computer languages may be hard for us to understand and read or they may be easy to understand. For example, "machine" language is probably the furthest removed from our own language because it deals in on/off signals. BASIC language, on the other hand uses many English-like commands, such as "GO TO; IF THEN." Generally, the further removed the language is from the machines binary processes, the slower the program will run. If you want a program to run quickly, it should be written in a low level language, but this makes it less portable and harder for other programmers to figure out. If you want a program to run on the widest number of different computers, a higher level language is recommended. Most programmers use a combination of both methods to write programs.

MENU-DRIVEN--Offers the user a list of instructions or messages so that an option may be chosen to perform various functions in a program. This is less flexible and slower than command-driven programs, yet easier to use. This is important in an environment in which many novice computer users need to access the computer.

SOFTWARE--The languages, programs, and processes of a computer system.

SOURCE CODE--A program written in its original computer language available to other programmers for modification and compilation. If a jeweler buys a canned program and desires to modify it, he will need to obtain the source code. The source code is the only means the software vendor has of controlling the distribution and modification of his software, it should not be a surprise to find that many software vendors will not provide a copy of a source code or that some will provide it but only at great expense to the buyer--even then the distribution of the software will be tightly controlled by contract making the jeweler liable if the source code falls into someone elses hands.

WORD PROCESSING--Tasks such as letter writing, printing, editing, and creating mailing lists carried out from a desktop terminal or computer.

Programming is both a craft and a science. Good programmers work for years to develop their programming styles. With the multitude of languages and computers available today, programmers often must learn more than one language to practice their profession.

It isn't necessary that you learn to program a computer before you are able to use one. If you had to rely on your own programming skills, jewelry business-related software would be years behind. In short, instead of developing new software, you would be better off learning how to apply the software already available to you

Even so, there is room for the development of jewelry software today. Many jewelers who have found a need to customize software to their own needs, have hired programmers to develop it for them or to modify commercially available programs. In doing so, they have been able to develop customized programs that fit their needs more closely than any unmodified, commercially available program could. And, to cover the developmental costs of new software, many of these jewelers later market it to others.

Still, in general, the most useful information you can know about computers is how to apply the programs that are now available. By knowing how to get the potential from the programs that are currently on the market, you'll have an arsenal of business tools at your disposal.

The most brawny programs available for business today have their own languages. These are called command driven programs. They are "driven" by a computer language which tells them how to proceed. Because of this specific language, you can spend many months learning these programs.

An alternative is the menu-driven program. A menu-driven program offers you the opportunity to choose options in the program from a "menu" that the computer puts up on its screen. When you select an option from the menu, the program will do those functions, and then present you with another menu from which to choose for further processing.

A command driven program does not have menus (although, by knowing the commands, you can create menus for it yourself). Rather, you must know the commands or choices in advance. The advantage of this style of program is its power and speed. The menu-driven program, while easier to use, is slower, weaker, and less flexible.

You can purchase a computer and a retail jewelry program, and, with no programming knowledge, you can be off and running. In general, the less you have to know to make the program work, the sooner you will be using it, but the less flexible it will be in meeting your needs. The ideal program, then, are those that maximize flexibility and ease of use -- the best of both styles.

COMMAND DRIVEN VERSUS MENU-DRIVEN

Figure 1.5.1

Researchers have estimated that the gap between computer literate and computer illiterate people will widen into the 1990's. Of those who do use computers, two groups of patrons exist: users and programmer. One estimate is that only 10% of the people involved in computing on a day-to-day basis are avidly involved in programming. The remaining 90% are users and operators.

Not everyone needs to know how to program. Programming requires individual mastery and long hours at the computer. For you, these are hours that can be used to sell diamonds; hours that, with the aid of your accountant, can be used to develop a financial model of your business on your electronic spreadsheet; hours during which you can make the maximum use of the existing jewelry and business-related software now on the market.

Yet, keep in mind that, whether you use the aid of a programmer or use canned applications, a niche does exist for you in generating applications for the jewelry business. For with sound knowledge of computers and software no one can create a jewelry related program more useful than a jeweler himself!

6

CANNED VS CUSTOM SOFTWARE

DISCUSSION OF TERMS

NETWORK--The connection of more than one computer for the purpose of sharing peripheral devices (such as printers, modems, hard disks, and so forth) and for distributed sharing of information including common data bases, inter and intra office mail, and telecommunication's information. Networks are usually connected to a file server in one of several topologies. The files server, which can be a mini-, mainframe, or microcomputer, usually has a hard disk drive and coordinates the activities of the network. Try to think of different computers tied together with either coaxial, twisted pair, or fiber optic cables. Methods are established to prevent the collision of information on the network. Future networks will tie together with the phone system and will be capable of binary, visual, and voice transmissions. Many networks can be joined together and when this happens, each network is called a node. By connecting computers in a network gives each computer in the network a greater capacity than it otherwise would have; this extra capability culminates in what can be best described as synergy -- a tool greater in its whole than in any anyone of its parts.

FILE SERVER--A computer used in a Local Area Network (LAN) as the mother node. The file server usually contains a hard disk, printer, and other input/output (I/O) devices. It may or may not be able to be used as a stand alone computer while it acts as the network server.

INPUT/OUTPUT DEVICE--Device such as a modem, printer, bar code reader, etc. that enables the computer to deal with the outside world.

VERTICAL SOFTWARE--Programs written for one industry -- each containing features useful to that particular business or industry.

What is software? The term software was originally invented to contrast with the term hardware, which was the iron or tangible materials involved in computers. Software is the languages, programs, and processes of the computer. A software package refers to one or more programs designed and documented to carry out one or more similar computer functions.

For example, most jewelers could benefit by having a word processing software package. With this you could compose letters more rapidly and send out professional looking correspondence.

Most software packages come with a manual that explains how to use the program. Program distributors normally distribute the software on magnetic storage devices called disks. The disk is read by the computer and the program is put into RAM (Random Read-Write Access Memory). These devices are similar to a stereo cassette tape in that the media are a magnetic storage device that holds the program in magnetic pulses on the tape. Although the shape and form of these media are of differing sizes, they all work by essentially the same process.

SOFTWARE AND HARDWARE EXAMPLES

Figure 1.6.1

Canned software has been developed to do a specific function. It has already been tested and debugged (a term that refers to removing any problems from the software. Its first use came in the 1950's when a technician troubleshooting a UNIVAC mainframe computer, the kind that takes up rooms of space, found a moth in a relay switch--alas the term de"bug"ging).

Normally a canned software package serves a general function. A few examples of canned business software would be accounts payable, accounts receivable, payroll, and general ledger. The cost of developing canned programs is shared by a larger market, spreading the cost of development over a wider user's base. Normally if you were to write such a program for your own use, it would be called a customized software program.

DE"BUG"ING

Figure 1.6.2

Should you buy a customized or canned package? Part of this answer may be obvious: are there any canned programs close to your needs? If so, it may make better sense to buy a canned program than to pay a programmer or a consultant to write a custom program for you. Of course, it is sometimes possible to buy a canned program and to also buy the source code for that program (source code is the program as written in the original computer language). With this source code, the consultant can tailor the program to your specifications. Some source codes are expensive, ie., thousands of dollars, whereas others are only several hundred dollars, and still others are not made available for any price.

If you are inclined to develop your own software, the software will generally closely match your business's requirements. If the result justifies the great expense of doing this, it may be just the thing for you. As more and more jewelers turn to computers, more packages will become available for you. In the computer industry, this evolution of programs for one industry, such as the jewelry business, is called vertical software development.

Currently, approximately 26 jewelry software programs exist. For the most part each one has accounts payable, accounts receivable, payroll, inventory control, and several other features (such as repair job control and layaway tracking, and sales analysis) on it. Most of these programs are available from various firms directly associated with the jewelry business.

You may find writing a vertical application the best path to choose. When developing software, you should try to defray the developmental costs by arranging a mutually beneficial deal with a programmer. Of course, it is a timely and expensive proposition for a programmer to develop an integrated software package for the jewelry business. It could take thousands of hours. Some programmers would not want to take on a project of such magnitude without periodic payments.

Most jewelry software houses (those who sell software and computers to the jewelry industry) will make modification in their programs at a modest fee. These houses specialize in providing both the equipment and software to you. You should look carefully at the amount of support these companies provide with their systems. Many of them will provide on-sight training; others require you and your staff to to go to the software house for training. These costs, which can be expensive, are usually provided in the contract that you sign when purchasing the software.

Jewelry software is quite specialized and sophisticated. Often times this additional training provided by the software house can be well worth the added expense. It save months of aggravation. Try looking at this as "hand holding." Until you are capable of riding the software bike on your own, the software house should ensure your safety by providing you with removable training wheels. For the particularly slow learner, additional training can be obtained at an additional fee.

Should you buy a jewelry software house's canned software or should you purchase more generic canned software? Several very good retail software packages are available but do not have jewelry industry specific segments, ie. appraisal, gold price, diamond price, jewelry tag, and computer aided jewelry design segments. These features can be most helpful to you, and can give you the boost you may need to enhance the productivity of your staff. Which ever one you choose, please remember that the computer that you buy is only as good as the software which runs on it. If you buy a jewelry software house's set of programs, be sure that the computer and its operating system don't leave you on the outside in terms of using other useful programs that may be available, but not for your computer.

More than two programs written specifically for jewelers run on the IBM Personal Computer (IBM PC). Although these programs were mostly written from scratch by their developers, these computers and the operating system on which these programs will run do permit the use of the over 5000 programs that are also available for this computer.

On the other hand, several other jewelry software houses who have been in existence for several years longer than the above mentioned firms, developed their packages for minicomputers and mainframe computers. Because these programs have been around for a much longer period of time, they contain far fewer bugs and more powerful and useful features in their jewelry related programs, however, they will not run the variety and quantity of other programs that will run on the IBM PC.

You probably know the IBM PC is a single-user computer and that the minicomputers are multi-user and multi-tasking computers. For that reason, if you require multiple computer terminals because your staff need to have simultaneous access to the computer then these minicomputer systems may be just what you need.

Recent developments have made the networking of microcomputers together a viable alternative to minicomputers. Very soon now, you will be able to hook together as many microcomputers as you need in your store. These computers will share common peripherals, ie. printers, hard disks, modems, and so forth. They will also allow you to perform separate tasks on different computers.

But, you say, this is possible right now. And so it is, but what happens on one microcomputer in the network if another user in the same network wants to access the same program and the same file at the same time? What happens right now if you don't want a parttime person to have access to the payroll information and to the account payable files?

On a minicomputer these files can only be accessed by someone who has a password. On a minicomputer two gemologists can not use the same file at the same time. This prevents the loss of information from the gemologist who doesn't save his information last. On a microcomputer network, as they are today you can not lock out the other gemologist from the same file and you can not realistically prevent a determined person from gaining access to a confidential file.

This is all about to change. Recent advances in microcomputer network technology will soon let you do all the above and more. In fact, these developments will probably be made available to users of most major microcomputers. That means that you will be able to buy one microcomputer with either generic accounting software or jewelry industry developed accounting software and know that as long as that software was designed to take advantage of the new networking technology that you may expand the number of computers in your store(s) without fear of losing control over the information and without having to buy a larger minicomputer to handle your growing needs.

It also means that you will now have the power of a minicomputer with over 5000 software packages available to you to meet your every computing need. Later, you will learn of the myriad of software tools that can carrying you beyond the "Second Ring".

7

SHOULD YOU HIRE A CONSULTANT?

Trying to learn a software package on your own, without the assistance of a professional can be dificult. Several jewelers I know have all incorporated various levels of assistance when choose a software package.

Who is a computer consultant? A computer consultant is an individual conversant in the applications and computer upon which you decide. Because of the many brands of computers and multitude of business software, many consultants have years of computer experience, but may often lack the specific knowledge on the programs you need or specific knowledge about your computer or information you consider important regarding your business. Most consultants, though, because of their years of experience are quick to pick up on your needs. In shopping for a consultant you should obtain the person best qualified to suit your needs. Instead of paying someone to learn your business, software, and computer, most experts agree that finding someone who already knows your computer, your business, and your software is better.

Of course, if you decide to buy a canned jewelry industry software package from one of the many vendors catering to your vertical market chances are that they will perform many of the functions that an independent computer consultant would perform, but you may find that an expert closer to home may provide some fresh insight into the operation of your newly automated business.

A consultant will help in the initial computer and software selection, guide you in setting up your computer, and train your people to use the new computer. If he is conversant in the language in which your program is written, the consultant can tailor a canned program to your needs, and he can trouble-shoot problems. The consultant can also develop additional software for your particular needs. Of course, all this will cost lots of money.

Depending on the experience level and education, fees vary from consultant to consultant. The fees can run

CALL IN A CONSULTANT WHEN YOU NEED HELP

Figure 1.7.1

from $200 to over $500 per day. In choosing a consultant, then, you should choose wisely, only using the consultant to do those tasks that you, yourself, can not do.

Frequently, especially for larger jewelry companies, it may be wiser to hire a knowledgeable computer expert for your staff. This person can be a programmer, a computer scientist, or an accountant with a computer background. Who it is depends on your needs and your extent of automation.

Word-of-mouth, yellow pages, advertisements in trade journals and computer magazines all advertise the services of computer consultants. Ideally, a consultant living nearby will be less expensive than one for whom you must pay travel and per diem expenses. Local colleges and universities can aid in locating a consultant to fit your needs.

One source of good information might be the local computer clubs in your own town. From here you can usually find one or more talented and eager computer experts. You can attend the club meetings; you may even pickup useful tips and additional business applications for your newly acquired software and computer. Computer clubs are sweeping the nation in popularity; you should have no problem locating one that covers your own brand of computer and software.

In some cities services exist that, for a percentage of the consultants fee, will find a consultant just right for the job. Often, consultants will sign up with the service to obtain freelance work. These services are a good clearing house for computer talent in the local area and should not be overlooked when seeking a computer expert.

Once you have located a consultant, you should not hesitate to put him to work. Ask lots of questions, too -- consultants know short cuts to solve data processing problems. If they do not know the answers, they know where to quickly locate them.

You will probably find that a consultant is needed more during the first phases of computerization, but do not hesitate to call on him at a later phase: he will be able to fine-tune an already well oiled operation.

Some consultants prefer to work under contract; while others prefer to be paid a lump sum for performing a defined task. Ultimately, it is more advantageous for you to provide detailed specifications to the consultant. From this, you can ask the prospective consultant to give an estimate of time and charges. If he overruns his established estimate, you should have a prior understanding with him on how to handle the additional time.

If the consultant is good and your specifications are adequate, he should be able to provide an accurate estimate of the time and price needed to complete the job.

Some consultants prefer to be put on a retainer; for an established fee they will make calls to your business on an "as needed" basis. If the visits do not exceed an established frequency limit, the consultant is there when you need him. This method does provide the consultant with a guaranteed monthly income.

Should you find that you have problems in obtaining results from the consultant, you can take several courses of action. Obviously, you can dismiss the consultant and hire another expert who will provide the desired services. In the end, though, the product that you receive from him is in large part determined by the amount of preparation and forethought you used in soliciting the services of the consultant. If you clearly establish your needs to the consultant, and once the consultant has clearly established his fee to deliver the service, then, in most cases, you can rest assured that you will receive the services for which you paid. If not, you can take the same actions that one of your own customers would take if he were not receiving satisfaction from you. That includes a formal complaint or arbitration up to and including legal action. Owing to the sensitive nature of automating the jewelry business, it is best to do your homework.

8

THE COMPUTER CONTRACT

DISCUSSION OF TERMS

TURNKEY SYSTEM--Situation in which a computer vendor supplies everything needed in one package -- hardware and software. The vendor would insure correct operation, installation, and service of the computer and its software. Turnkey systems generally meet a very specific need of the customer and perform that job quite well. Most turnkey systems involve minicomputer systems but, of late, many developers are creating turnkey systems for microcomputers.

Whether you decide to go with a propriety software company or a canned jewelry program or whether you decide to choose a minicomputer or a microcomputer, depends in part on the total package you choose. Most software is designed to run on usually one brand of computer. Thus, you will be locked into a computer hardware choice if you decide on a specific computer software package. The opposite is also true.

This tie-in is often called a turnkey system -- when a

software package and a computer are sold as one package. In this manner the computer vendor supplies everything in one package to insure the correct operation of your software. Because of this interwoven nature of software, service, and hardware, you should take legal precautions when the risks become large.

When should you insist upon a contract? Table 1.8.1 gives you some guidelines.

IF YOU ANTICIPATE SPENDING OVER $15,000
IF THE SOFTWARE COSTS OVER $5,000
IF THE SOFTWARE WAS CUSTOM MADE
IF THE JEWELER PLANS TO EXPAND IN THE FUTURE WITH THE SAME EQUIPMENT
IF THE JEWELER'S RISKS ARE VERY HIGH BECAUSE OF THE NATURE OF THE INFORMATION THAT HE WILL KEEP ON THE COMPUTER

WHEN DO YOU NEED A CONTRACT

Table 1.8.1

Of course, these are only suggestions about when you should seek the aid of legal counsel and the protection of a legal contract. If you plan to spend a lot of money to automate, your business is at risk; the greater the risk, the greater your protection should be.

What should you look for in a computer contract? Foremost, you should be sure that the contract includes a specific list of the hardware the vendor or consultant is to provide. For example, is a modem included? Will a printer be included? What size is it? Who makes it? What style is it? How many terminals are included?

Further, when will the equipment arrive? When is it scheduled to be on line for your use? What happens if there is a delay or cost increase? Are you protected against unscheduled cost increases? Also, what is the cost of all equipment and software including all fees from installation through software development? Lastly, how will you be expected to pay for it?

COMPARE BEFORE BUYING

Figure 1.8.1

Another important item in the contract is the guarantee. Is there a guarantee? Who and what is supported by it? What if the vendor does not live up to his agreement? What length of time does the guarantee cover? Make sure you have answers to these questions long before any problem arises.

The contract should also cover the key items you relied upon in choosing the hardware and software that you are buying or leasing. This will make clear what your expectations are.

Lastly, what happens if the agreement doesn't work out? What can you do to recoup your expenses? Of course no one can ever foresee all the legal ramifications in a venture as complex as computerizing a jewelry store, but through proper planning and a good contract you will be better prepared to receive your computer system, and to deal with a faulty agreement if that becomes necessary.

- PART 2 -

THE IDEAL JEWELRY PROGRAM

INTRODUCING THE IDEAL JEWELRY PROGRAM

Why should we be concerned with an "ideal" program for automating jewelry stores? Plenty of canned and customized packages exist for the jewelers use already. Would not one of those do?

For the jeweler who can afford those programs, the answer is yes. But, because many of those programs have not been developed specifically for jewelers, the cost of adapting them to your business will be high.

By looking, then, at a "wish list" of sorts for jewelry business computer applications, I will show you what you will ultimately expect in the future of computerization for your business.

This ideal, the Ideal Jewelry Program (I.J.P.), does not exist in whole -- at least not yet, and not as a total package. But, the majority of the programs and "segments" it contains are available to you today. And, with recent developments in the microcomputer marketplace, I expect that only a brief period stands between now and the time when most of these features will be packaged in a total program for the jeweler.

Much of the technology needed to do that sort of "software packaging" for jewelers is here today. And, when our industry sees and integrated, inexpensive and modular computer program that will run on an inexpensive, standardized and portable computer system, automation will become far easier for all of us.

It will become a case of supply and demand. As more and more jewelers computerize, improved and standardized software will become available that is designed with their special needs in mind. For now, the I.J.P. will show you individual "bits and pieces" of that kind of software. With the exception of "3-D Graphics Diamond Analysis," the "Gemologist's Workbench," and the "Interactive Computer-aided Jewelry Design program" these are programs you find today -- ones that have already been developed for retailers and others -- which you can adapt for your use.

Remember, the computer is a tool that will help increase profits. Just like advertising, just like window displays, just like one-year guarantees, and just like the jeweler's torch, the computer will see us into the year 2000 and beyond. As the following chapters on the I.J.P. expose you to the many uses of the computer, think about how these programs could fit into you business. Because, after finishing this part of the book, you will know precisely what a computer will do for you today . . . and in the future.

Welcome to the Ideal Jewelry Program.

JEWELER'S TOOLS

1

INTEGRATION & STANDARDIZATION

DISCUSSION OF TERMS

"C" LANGUAGE--A portable and powerful computer language that is used to develop many of todays integrated programs. It was developed by Bell Laboratories.

INTEGRATION--An elusive concept in programming that uses a common command syntax throughout the various modules of a program. Data can be transferred more freely and easier than with non-integrated programs. There are varying degrees of integration. Ultimately, the greatest degree of compatibility to other programs while retaining an integrated nature should be the design of an integrated package.

Because of the nature of an integrated package, the programs in unison are greater than anyone individual segment -- this is again the synergy I spoke of earlier. An integrated program should fit around the jeweler like the car that is built around the driver. It should make his life easier and provide an extremely powerful tool in the daily affairs of business. It should be easy to learn, but not too easy. It should be both command and menu driven. This allows the more experienced user to by-pass familiar menus.

Integration can be obtained through an external means of an integrating style oparating system like IBM's "Top-view" and Microsoft's "Windows" or it can provide a series of segments that act like one program such as Ashton-Tate's "Framework" and Lotus' "Symphony". Program's that run under the UNIX operating system can be said to have an integrated nature, although this is more a result of UNIX than of the program itself. What will be nice to see are programs such as "Symphony" and "Framework" run under the UNIX operating system.

Because of the dual nature of the I.J.P, from the standpoint of its inherent accounting functions and because of its specialized and integrated nature, it will provide the jeweler with a tool for profitability and for productivity. He might try doing his administrative functions with out the use of the I.J.P. but will find that his life is easier when he uses the I.J.P.

PC DISK OPERATING SYSTEM (PC DOS)-- An operating system developed by Microsoft of Bellevue, WA. It is the standard operating system used on the IBM PC line of computers. Version 3.1 is the networking operating system that was mentioned in Part One that has opened the door to using several IBM PC compatible computers in a jewelry store. The advantage to using it is that not only do powerful accounting programs run under it, but that over 6,000 additional programs will run under it, too. Many of these programs provide a jeweler with ways of looking at his business in such new and novel way than heretofore thought possible. Previous versions of DOS did not have networking capabilities.

TOPVIEW--An IBM software program that enables the IBM series of Personal Computers to run software in a manner that makes the sharing of data and commands between programs more of a reality than myth. Other programs have entered the market place but have failed to capture the hearts and minds of the majority of IBM PC users. TOPVIEW gives the IBM PC and AT a multi-tasking capability.

UNIX--An operating system developed by AT&T that is multi-user and multi-tasking and is portable from computer to computer. It consists of over 200 utility programs that can be combined in such a synergistic manner that often precludes the need for other more specialized programs. UNIX uses pipes and filter (electronic) to perform many of these advanced and useful functions. Although UNIX was developed at Bell Laboratories and at major universities in an academic environment, it is the only operating system capable of running on the greatest variety of mini-, micro-, and mainframe computers. It was written in the "C" language, which explains its portability and speed of operation. More and more businesses are turning to turnkey systems based on the UNIX operating system.

Integration, the capability of sharing data among programs and of using a common command syntax among programs, is the hallmark of the Ideal Jewelry Program. By integrating the jewelry program functions from accounts payable through inventory control, it will be able to show you the connection between all of your data -- how each function you do relates to all others. And, by providing this connection -- this integration -- it will mean that all of your data will need to be entered only once in order to have it affect all of the "segments" of the I.J.P.

For example, let us assume that John Hillary, a good customer, has purchased a $3000 necklace. He put it on your store's charge account. Which of your records will this single transaction affect?

First, Mr. Hillary needs an appraisal of the necklace. Then, he has to be billed for his purchase on a monthly statement -- so accounts receivable will have to be posted. Third, inventory records have to be reduced by one necklace. And, if the necklace was on memo, billing has to be requested and accounts payable posted appropriately. Fifth, because you found out the date of Mr. Hillary's anniversary and his wife's birthday, you should record this in the customer data base on your computer.

About the same time, another of your stores requests the same necklace. You'd have to be able to notify them that it was sold and that another one has been requested on memorandum. And, a Thank You note should go out to Mr. Hillary. Lastly, the sales report and daily ledger have to be posted.

If you're not computerized, chances are good that you'd have to post and take care of all of these many functions separately. In an integrated computer program, all of this data will need to be handled only once. The program will automatically post all records, including a print-out of that thank you not for the salesperson's signature.

In addition to being integrated, the Ideal Jewelry Program will also be standardized. Because of its complex nature, it will need to be created to run on a computer powerful enough to handle the size of a program that will do all of this, flexible enough to satisfy your needs, but inexpensive enough to be affordable. It will be simple and, if you didn't need all those segments, it will be modularized so that you will use the parts of your choice. Later, if necessary, you will move up to other segments. To accomplish all of this,we turn to the concept of standardization.

In order for the I.J.P. to become a standard in and of itself, it will need to be created for a standardized microcomputer operating system. Some powerful and flexible jewelry software programs like this do exist, but they leave off where affordability comes in. Because, for the most part, they are not standards -- they are not available on a standardized computer or operating system.

For the I.J.P. to acquire this sort of standardization, it will need to be written in a portable language, such as "C", and on a powerful and portable operating system, such as UNIX or on a networkable, standardized operating system such as MS DOS (version 3.1 or higher).

To understand this, lets look at the following. Until recently, a standardized microcomputer operating system did not exist in the computer field. Today, IBM has introduced its line of personal computers: the IBM PC, the

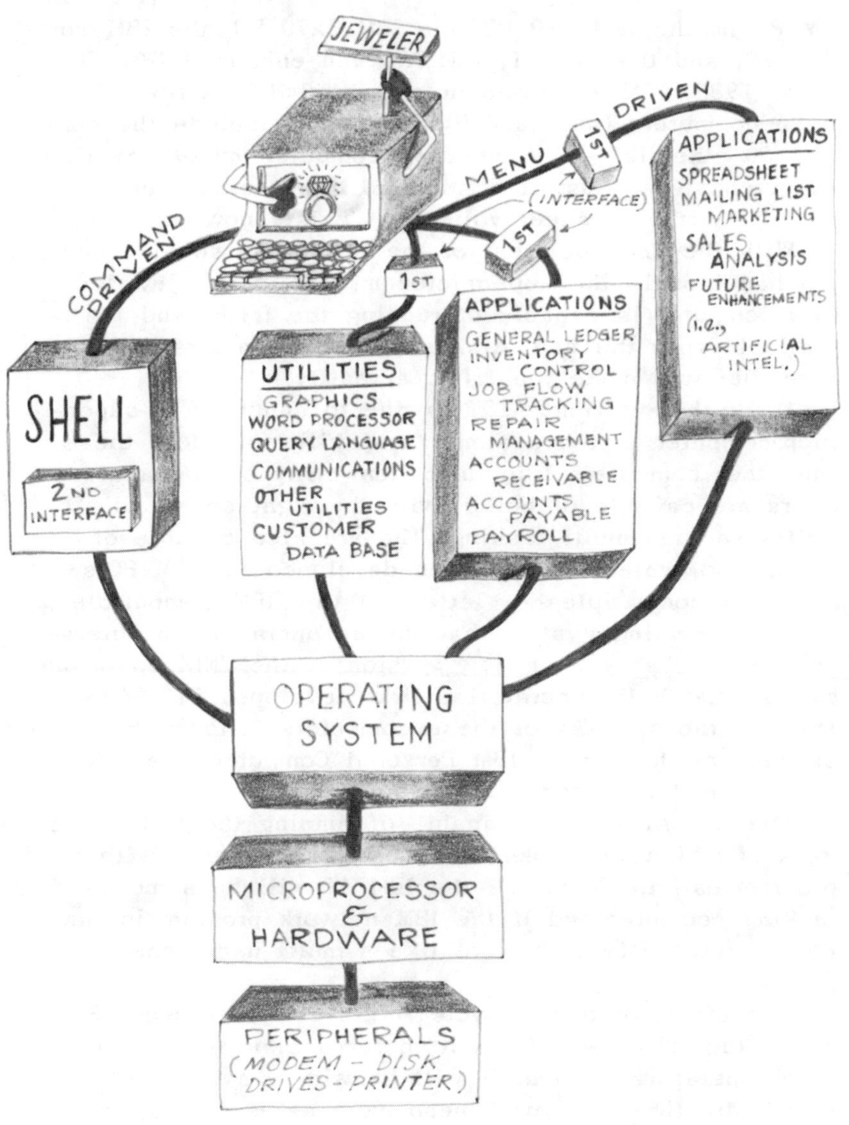

IDEAL JEWELRY PROGRAM

Figure 2.1.1

IBM PC jr, the IBM-370 PC, the IBM 3270 PC, the IBM Portable PC, and the IBM XT, IBM AT, and enhanced IBM AT.

By 1985, IBM had sold an estimated 3.5 million of these computers (and this figure doesn't include the more than 50 other IBM PC compatible computer models available for purchase). Thus, if a standard didn't exist before this, by virtue of sheer volume, it exists now.

With the announcement of the IBM AT personal computer, IBM has brought the supermicrocomputer to the Jeweler. This computer is capable of running the I.J.P. and is available with the hard disk storage and integrated software that will make the I.J.P. a reality.

As of this writing, AT&T is due to announce a supermicrocomputer that has similar capabilities. Both these and other computers like them from many other manufacturers are capable of being (with the right software) multi-user and multi-tasking. The are also capable of running software that has been developed for IBM PC's and their compatibles -- let's call this IBM compatible.

The operating system that these supermicrocomputers use will probably be a new version of the UNIX operating system that Bell Laboratories first developed in 1969. Thus, if the success of these computers follows the success of the earlier IBM Personal Computer, they, too, are destined to become a standard.

The IBM AT is also capable of running the IBM PC network of which we spoke in an earlier chapter. With a program called "Topview", the IBM AT will be a multi-tasking computer and if the IBM network program is run concurrently, it will behave like a multi-user computer.

The effect of this on your future computer use? Because the I.J.P. will be written for a standardized computer operating system, it will be widely available -- standardization of it will mean more sales. This, in turn, means reduced software prices, and that will make the I.J.P. more affordable for all jewelers.

UNIX...A PORTABLE, POWERFUL OPERATING SYSTEM

Figure 2.1.2

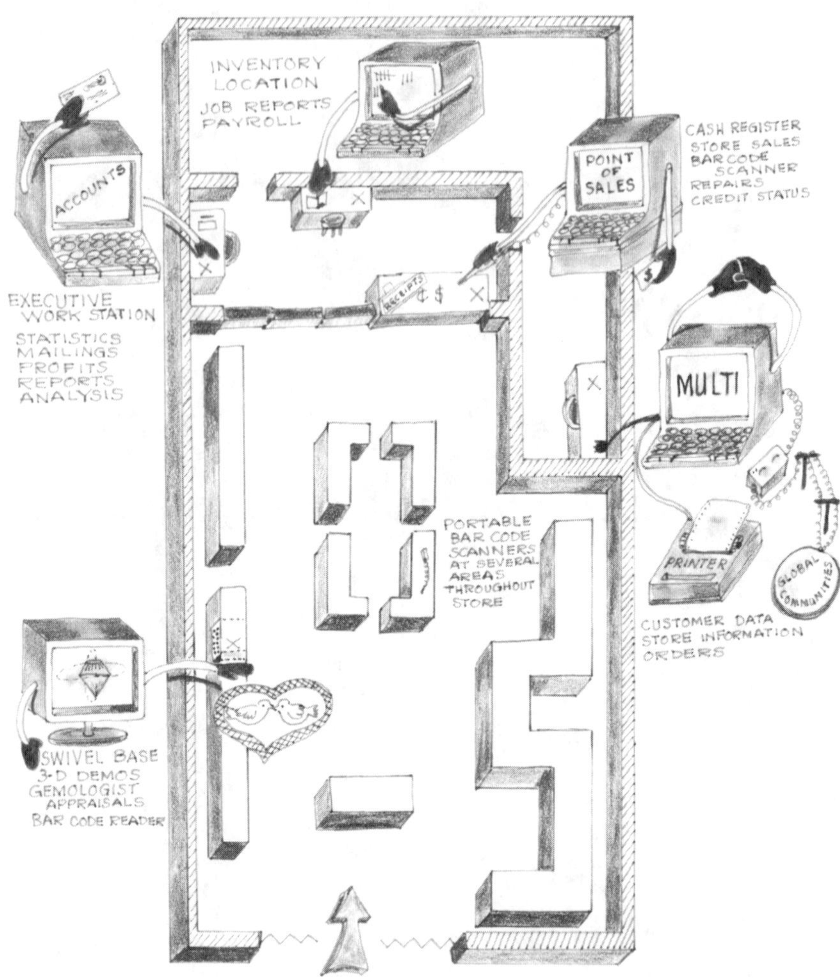

COMPUTER USAGE IN A JEWELRY STORE

Figure 2.1.3

2

TELECOMMUNICATIONS

DISCUSSION OF TERMS

DOWNLOAD--Receiving data from another computer into a target computer via a serial or parallel port. Infers from you to me.

ELECTRONIC MAIL--The replacement of inter and intra office paper correspondence through the use of computers and software specially designed to accommodate the greater throughput potential of electronic data.

MODEM--A modulator-demodulator device that converts digital signals into telephone language and back to digital signals.

OPEN-TO-BUYS--A budget established by the jeweler allocating dollars available for inventory based on anticipated sales. It protects the jeweler from overspending dollars on excess inventory during low sale periods.

STOCK TURN--Term used to indicate the amount of times that merchandise sells in a given period of time. One popular formula is

$$\frac{\text{sales at cost}}{\text{average inventory at cost}}$$

TELECOMMUNICATE--A means of transferring data through electrical means, ie. telephone and radio. Computers are capable of transferring vast quantities of information through telecommunications.

UPLOAD--Sending data to another computer. Infers from me to you.

Telecommunications, the passing of information by electrical means, is here to stay. With the I.J.P., you will have the means to communicate by computer. If you have a store in another city, you will be able to send and receive data between computers. Be it inventory records, sales receipt information, employee records, electronic mail, or current diamond prices, you will transfer these data and more.

For one computer to talk with another requires a modulator-demodulator device called a modem. The computer hooks up to the modem via a serial port, an input/output (I/O) device (through which the computer talks with the outside world) on the computer. The modem then transforms machine's language of bits into electrical signals that can be transmitted over the phone lines. At the receiving end, the modem converts the electrical signals back into bits.

Modems run at varying speeds. The quality of the telephone line or wire dictates the speed at which the computer can transfer information. For voice grade telephone lines (the telephone lines that we normally use), the speed is usually limited to about 1200 baud. Baud is the number of discrete signaling units per second; therefore, 1200 baud means that the computer, through its serial port, hooked into its modem, can transfer 1200 separate signals a second. As speed increases over 1200 baud, the quality of the transmission wire should improve also. For faster speeds, a dedicated line is necessary to prevent signal losses. The average person would not have a problem reading data at 300 baud; 1200 baud would be too fast to read.

Modems are available for most computers, today. Two basic types exist, acoustic and direct connect modems. The acoustic modem has to be manually connected to a phone receiver and it relies on sound waves to transfer signals from the modem to the phone. The direct connect modem is wired directly to the phone. Serious users prefer the direct connect modem, and in the business environment, it will be the preferred method. Soon, modem circuitry will be available on one microprocessor. When this happens, the price of modems will drop dramatically and their speeds will increase. For now, however, the faster the modem is, the more expensive it is.

More sophisticated modems can automatically answer and dial. In the I.J.P., you will be able to go home in the evening, leave your computer on, your modem on, and receive phone calls from your other store(s), uploading (receiving) and downloading (sending) data. You will also have access to your computer from your home via a home computer. Of course, a password or other security measure should be in effect to insure no unauthorized users tamper with your computer and its data.

Why should you, as a jeweler, be concerned with telecommunications?

A major jewelry retail leasing company now uses a modem and keyboard to transfer daily sales information and inventory figures from throughout its many leased jewelry departments to its corporate headquarters.

Let's look at a future example. Soon, salespeople will call on you, take an inventory of your merchandise in stock, input the inventory into their portable computers, connect it to the phone, and upload the inventory data to their parent company's computer. Within seconds the salesperson will receive output back from his company. From that data, he will know your total dollars spent, the total items sold, the dollar value of goods sold, and a recommended buying plan to help improve your stock turn. The salesperson will also know what items in his line have been dropped, any new items for sale, and the current on-hand stock at the factory.

At this point, if you are using the Ideal Jewelry Program, you will already know, through your own computerized inventory system, how many of the salesperson's products sold (might the real reason for the salesperson coming to your store be to present new jewelry styles?) Before the salesperson's visit, you will have ordered all the high stock turn items saving only a part of your open-to-buy dollars for any new styles presented.

Besides giving the manufacturer a grasp of what his products will be doing in your jewelry store, the above scenario will give you much tighter control over your spending. Needlessly spending money on inventory that doesn't turnover is costly. Identifying and then stocking stock turn items reduces your inventory investment, while at the same time improving your sales potential. In time, most manufacturers may make available to you a means to order jewelry directly, from computer to computer. Some manufacturers may even find it cost effective to buy a computer, including software, for a retail jewelry firm, if the jeweler guarantees a specific dollar volume over a specified period. The net savings incurred by both the manufacturer and the jeweler may make this symbiotic relationship possible. With communications software, modems, and computers, this may soon begin.

3

PUBLIC INFORMATION NETWORKS

DISCUSSION OF TERMS

BAUD--The number of discrete signaling units per second used in determining the speed at which a computer can transmit information.

BINARY CODE--Or machine language--Code made up of two different values assigned to each code element.

COMPUSERVE--An on-line textual data base system that contains data covering a very broad base of topics, ie. diamond prices, commodities and stocks, Special Interest Groups (SIG), and so forth. Compuserve can be accessed through communication software, a modem, and telephone lines. Compuserve charges the user actual connect time.

CONNECT TIME--The time a person actually spends connected to a telecommunication network or on a time-sharing computer, which is a computer that keeps track of time spent on the system for billing purposes. Time sharing also denotes a multi-user computer system in which all users share the computer for time of the central processor.

NORTH AMERICAN PRESENTATION LEVEL PROTOCOL SYNTAX (NAPLPS) -- A symbolic system of coding videotext images so that they can be transferred easily and quickly on telecommunication networks, ie. phones and so forth.

ON-LINE--Denotes currently in use or over a telecommunications network, ie. He is on-line with his other store or the on-line data base contains information that I can give you as soon as I have received it.

PROMPT--Being coached or reminded to perform a predefined task. On a computer, one is often prompted to press a key or take certain prescribed steps.

SPECIAL INTEREST GROUP (SIG)--In a computer club or on an on-line data base such as Compuserve or the Source, it is a group of people who are interested in one computer related topic and who meet (in person or on-line) to share information about this topic. In a computer club, an example would be the new member SIG; on Compuserve, a SIG would be all IBM Personal Computer users.

VIDEOTEXT--Term describing the systems used to provide services such as homebanking, shopping, business information, news, weather, and so forth, to homes and businesses. The systems use either telephone connections (viewdata) or unused television broadcast signals. Videotext also is used by many as a replacement word for Viewdata.

VIEWDATA--Offers services similar to videotext, but uses a telephone connection instead of broadcast signals. The viewer can send and receive information via a remote control hand-held keypad.

Videotext and viewdata networks will be the second reason for the Ideal Jewelry Program to have telecommunications capabilities.

VIDEOTEXT

The North American Presentation Level Protocol Syntax (NAPLPS), videotext, now popular in Canada, Europe, and Japan, uses unused portions of the video signal on a television set. NAPLPS is a standardized means of coding graphics so that they can be transmitted among different brands of computers. While still unsophisticated, videotext offers homebanking, homeshopping, and information services. In some respects, it follows the basic format of the viewdata networks (which are explained below); although it allows a more graphic representation than viewdata services.

The future looks bright for videotext services. IBM, Sears, and AT&T recently announced plans for a joint videotext service.

VIEWDATA

Viewdata, originally developed in England by the British Postal Services, utilizes the telephone line, a computer terminal, and a monitor or television set. A two-way, interactive communication network, its services include retail goods, airline information, Electronic Mail, encyclopedias, Stock Market and commodity services, professional information networks, special interest groups, and more. Table 2.3.1 provides a partial list of these viewdata electronic data bases. Videotext, a general term, often includes viewdata as a subcategory and will be used for both meanings, although viewdata does not use the NAPLPS standard but rather the American Standard Code for Information Exchange (ASCII), which does not include sophisticated graphic symbols of the NAPLPS.

How will this affect you? Jewelers who sell by mail-order today, if they are smart, will sell by videotext tomorrow. Compuserve, a videotext service, offers diamond trading services to members of the jewelry trade. For a first time fee of $39.50 and an on-line fee from less than $10 to more than $20 per hour, a jeweler can subscribe to Compuserve. By first signing up with the Rapaport Diamond Company (RDC), you will receive instant updates on the New York diamond market. The RDC lists all diamond sizes, shapes, prices, colors, and clarities. It even lists whether the diamond comes with a laboratory certificate or not. Also available is a current buy-and-sell listing of diamonds that RDC either has in stock or for which it has a buy request. Besides diamond prices, RDC provides information to the public on the history and grading of diamonds (diamond price information is reserved for members of the trade). The RDC refreshes its database daily and features electronic mail permitting a 24- hour, 7-day-per-week access with the RDC.

Bibliographic Retrieval Service
Compuserve
Dialogue
Dow Jones News Retrieval Service
E-COM
ELHILL LEXIS
Medlars
NEXIS
Orbit
The Source

Public Videotext Services

Table 2.3.1

The Gemological Research Corporation, San Mateo, California, headed by David Beare, offers the GemNet, a million dollar inventory of loose gemstones on a computer database. For a membership fee of $100, you can buy and sell gemstones on GemNet.

These services give real-time inventories of diamonds and colored stones. Due to the standardization of diamond grading practices and the impending standardization of colored stone grading practices, these videotext services will give you access to millions of dollars in inventory. You will be able to download the dealer's inventory into your own computer, providing you with a listing of all available gemstones. You will no longer need to call two, three, four, or more gem firms to find the one stone your customer wants. You will know its availability and its cost. Also, you could put your own gemstones on the networks for other dealers and other jewelers to buy.

What are some disadvantages to these systems? If the System Operators (SYSOP) of these gemstone trading services make their services available outside the jewelry industry, it will lead to the trading of diamonds and colored stones as commodities. The less romance (romance, as I use it, refers to the general mystique that surrounds the history, lore, and social customs associated with diamonds and gemstones) plays a part in the consumer's decision to buy gemstones, the greater the likelihood that gemstones will be treated as commodities. If romance is to stay an integral part of the jewelry business, then, jewelers and gemstone suppliers will have to control access to dealer priced databases. Furthermore, because of each gem's distinctive nature, these services will never give the unique advantage that seeing the gem will provide to its buyer.

As videotext becomes more sophisticated and as gemstone grading becomes more automated and standardized, however, the jewelry industry may nurture a strong trading tool. Today, computers will generate sophisticated graphics, but this is at the expense of computer memory and dollars. When videotext networks begin to paint high resolution graphic displays of diamonds and colored stones at a reasonable cost, tele-gem-buying will become a workable reality.

To better understand this, we will take a look at how such a system works in another field. Professional photographers can sign up with a national computer link called PhotoNet. As a member of this videotext service, a photographer has access to assignments and professional information. Editors, publishers, and others requiring the services of a photographer can request these on PhotoNet. The System Operator (SYSOP) of the Data Base places geographic and professional data about each member photographer on the database. Any photographer that responds to the requesting editor can take on the assignment for an agreed upon fee.

Today, the American Gem Society, the Accredited Gemologist Association, and others, strive to standardize the qualifications for jewelry appraisers. All of these organizations could start similar services, like PhotoNet, on a videotext network that give the public the names, qualifications, and business addresses of the qualified appraisers and member stores in their area. In addition to receiving royalties (most of these services charge for connect time and pay a fee based on usage to the SYSOP) from the Network Operator, these organizations would benefit from the positive public exposure.

Further, a videotext network based on gemological and jewelry related data could be created to which any gemologist, jeweler, or supplier could subscribe. The latest in gemological developments will always be available to you. Standardized markup structures and price aids will also be included that will aid appraisers in standardizing appraisal prices and procedures. For example, inputting over the phone to the other computer the refractive index, specific gravity, and other data, you will obtain the possible identification of an unidentified gemstone. This network will even prompt you through the steps of a gem identification. As artificial intelligence becomes a reality, a gemological expert system will be created that gives jewelers having access to

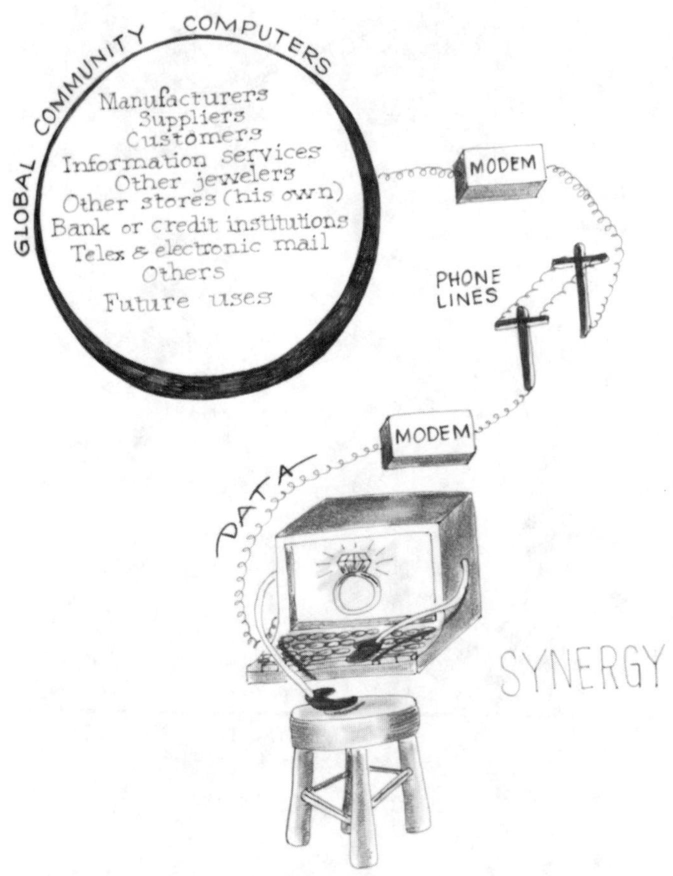

JEWELER'S GLOBAL COMMUNITY

Figure 2.3.1

the network the skill of a highly-trained gemologist -- and all for the price of a phone call.

More can be done via telecommunications. But, to summarize, the computer gives you access to a global community; it is changing the way we now do business. In the I.J.P., communications will play an integral role in providing a direct link between the supplier, the jeweler, and the customer.

4

THE CUSTOMER DATA BASE

DISCUSSION OF TERMS

MAILMERGE--Capacity of a word processor to use a mailing list data base to create letters containing personalized information. This name is also a trademark of the Compupro Company for their Mailmerge program.

The increasing power and long term storage capacity of computers today will make the Customer Data Base a reality.

The more you know about your customers, the greater the effectiveness of your direct mail campaigns. The I.J.P. will give you the ability to store and retrieve information about each of your customers. The information will include the areas shown in Table 2.4.1.

Of course, you will build this information over time. How will you collect it? One way will be to send out personal, confidential questionnaires to your list of customers. Did you know that when George Gallop takes a poll about any topic, he generally queries about 1,250 people? Certainly, his techniques require vast statistical know-how, however, you don't need to be a statistician to asks your customers to volunteer the information in Table 2.4.1. With the information that you request, you will begin to create a picture of your clientele. Through the use of mailmerge and word processing programs you can send customized mailing directed personally, by name, to each of your customers.

Name
Sex
Income
Types of Business
Number of Children
Past Jewelry Purchased
Amount of Purchase
Date of Purchases
Date of Last Appraisal
Age
Wife's or Husband's Birthday
Anniversary Dates
Zip Codes
Phone Numbers
Address
Birthplace
Birthdate
Schools Attended
Salesperson Who Sold Them
Additional Information
Life Cycle Ending Date

Sample of Customer Information

Table 2.4.1

Let me explain. Many word processors allow for the creation of customized letters that will selectively draw upon certain "what if" scenarios. For example, lets say that you wanted to write a letter telling all your 39 year old housewives who all had college degrees from Eastern United States universities about a new style of jewelry that was just developed in Maine. To reach this segment of your clientele you will need to know how many of them meet these specifications. Because you will have collected this information on your clientele in the Customer Data Base, you only need to merge those names into a customized letter directly addressed to each of these women. Imagine that you have a LASER printer, which will print at speeds up to 8 pages per minute and which produces a type-set looking letter. Even though it may take you an hour, imagine again that you personally sign each of these letters. Imagine that each of these customers receives your letter and that it brings to each of them a memory of fond times now past. But because of this memory that you conjured up in your clients, ten of them purchased the item of jewelry of which you spoke.

Perhaps this sounds far-fetched, but is it?

Fifty-five percent of the people who receive direct mail advertising read it. Above all other advertising media, direct mail is the most flexible and aims most directly at individuals. A person who reads direct mail advertisements usually gives it their undivided attention. And, to derive the greatest help from direct mail advertising, it must be targeted to a particular market group.

MAILING LIST

The mailing list will be created from a directory of addresses that can be selectively printed on labels or on envelopes. The Customer Data Base is one pool from which these names will be taken. You can select the criteria for the Mailing List from any category of the Customer Data Base.

For example, suppose you wanted to send a man's watch

brochure to all male customers over the age of 30 with an income of greater than $35,000 per year. You will query your Customer Data Base for just those customers. The program will print out the labels or envelopes on your printer.

By informing your customers when their appraisals needed updating, you will use the Customer Data Base to generate more appraisal business.

You can make a weekly or monthly list of all your customers whose birthdays or anniversaries fall within that period of time. You can call husbands at their offices, making a gift suggestion for their wives' birthday or anniversary; you can call wives at home or work suggesting a gift for their husbands' upcoming birthday or anniversary.

Further, you can use it to determine qualified leads (a customer who has already been introduced to your reputation and products, and who has a need for a similar product again). Each of their products has a life cycle; many engagement rings will need a new shank or prongs in 5 to 15 years. Usually two months prior to the end of the product's life cycle is the most advantageous time for the jeweler to put himself in front of the customer. Let's explain. The Customer Data Base will provide a listing of all the products your customers have bought. It will include what was purchased, how much, how many, and to whom it was given, if this was known at the time. Further, you will know the date on which the jewelry was purchased. Knowing the date you will be able to ascertain, with a reasonable degree of accuracy, the end of the life cycle. You can, assuming you have been in business for at least one life cycle, query your computer for a listing of all customers whose engagement ring life cycles will be ending within two months.

With the listing in hand you will call these customers, ask them if they were still happy with the product, remind them about your free cleaning and inspection program, describe any new engagement styles you recently received, and invite the customer to return to your store. This aggressiveness, although tamed and discrete, will assuredly generate greater buying traffic.

The Customer Data Base will be a powerful tool; yet, it will require constant maintenance. To grow it will have to be fertilized with additional customers, and weeded when their personal data changes. The Customer Data Base, together with the Mailing List feature of the I.J.P. will give you the means to magnify the personalized nature of your business. In today's competitive market place, this may be the edge you need to gain or recapture a greater part of your market.

ONE...SALE COULD HAVE BEEN... FOUR
THERE IS A NEED FOR MORE CUSTOMER INFORMATION

Figure 2.4.1

5

THE COMPUTER AS A WORD PROCESSOR

DISCUSSION OF TERMS

CUT-AND-PASTE--Process of transferring and integrating data with the use of windows. It can also be called "using a clipboard". It also means moving blocks of text to other areas of text in a word processing file. Writers and editors would usually cut and paste pieces of paper that contained paragraphs and sentences from a written document until it was shaped into the final manuscript or document.

LASER PRINTER--A printer that uses a laser beam and a complex series of reflectors and refractors that is capable of producing high resolution graphics and text at speeds in excess of 300 characters per second. The quality is significantly better than most other computer printers. Many laser printers use copier technology to produce the final image. Prices of these printers have come down to a level that jewelers can finally afford, but they are still at least twice as expensive as most printers on the market. The print in this book was set using a Corona Laser Printer (Model LP-300).

WINDOWS--Portions of memory data displayed in overlapping sections on a screen at one time. These can be different programs or different parts of the same program. It facilitates the user in dealing with a multi-tasking environment. Most windowing programs attempt to integrate the transfer of data from one program to the other. The common input/output (i/o) device used in windowing is the mouse. Windowing is the direction MS DOS is taking to make it a multi-tasking environment. Some windowing programs allow more than one application to run in the foreground and other in the background. Yet others only allow one program to run at a time while only displaying (not running) parts of other tasks in underlying windows.

WORD PROCESSING SOFTWARE--The programs available that are geared specifically to word processing applications.

WORD PROCESSOR--The desktop unit consisting of a display screen, keyboard and printer that uses software programs to perform word processing tasks.

On today's microcomputer software market, four major uses of the computer stand out: Word Processing, Spreadsheet or "What-If" analysis, Data Base Management, and Communications. Of these, word processing will give you a tool to produce professional looking correspondence and personalized mailings, prepare reports, employee manuals, appraisals, and job descriptions. In any task in which you will have to manipulate the written word, the word processor will do it more quickly, neater, and better than by hand or typewriter.

As part of word processing, printers transfer the print from the computer to paper. The daisy wheel printer is slowest but provides typewriter quality print. The dot-matrix printer is fast (usually from 80 to 400 characters per second) and will approach the quality of the daisy wheel printer. The ink jet printer is quiet, fast, and rivals the daisy wheel printer in quality. Lastly, the laser printer is versatile, extremely fast, capable of high quality print, but expensive (for example, this book was set with a laser printer).

If you have a lot of correspondence, having two printers will be best: the daisy wheel for correspondence and the dot-matrix for all others. If you are flush with money, produce as much correspondence as the State Government, and needs a high quality graphics printer, the laser printer will be the perfect choice! Soon, however, laser printers will be as inexpensive as a good daisy wheel printer.

In the I.J.P., the word processor will be integrated with all the other segments, ie. Payroll, Appraisals, Communications, Accounts Receivable, and so forth. The word processor will take the input from these segments and convert them into printable reports. The program will capture diamond and colored stone diagrams and print them on appraisal forms.

A window divides the monitor screen into different areas. Imagine a series of tiles overlapping each other with the top one being the file now in use. Also, imagine being able to reduce or enlarge the size of this tile so that it either takes up the entire screen or is overlapped by the other tiles. Each window will be a tile of the I.J.P.. For example, when the word processor is the top tile or window, data from the accounts payable segment of the I.J.P. can be brought into the letter that you are typing to your accountant. This eliminates the need to manually retype this data into the letter; time is saved, and the correspondence is made to look professional.

The word processor will use windows (looking at different segments of the same file or to look at different files at the same time). Advanced word processors will look at up to seven windows at one time. To understand how a word processor works, imagine the computer as a typewriter. The monitor will be the paper, the computer's cursor the striker. With a word processor the typist has total control over the placement of the cursor on

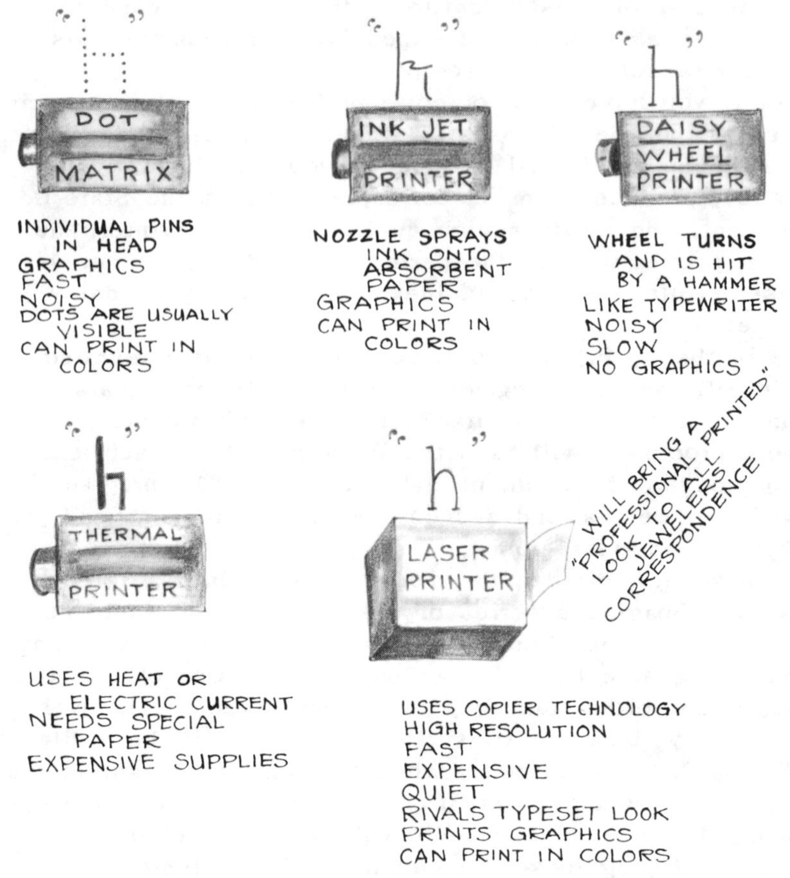

VARIETY OF PRINTERS

Figure 2.5.1

the monitor. The typist will add, delete, move, exchange words and letters and paragraphs from place to place in the file (the current document being typed). With windows, the typist will see and move more than one file at one time.

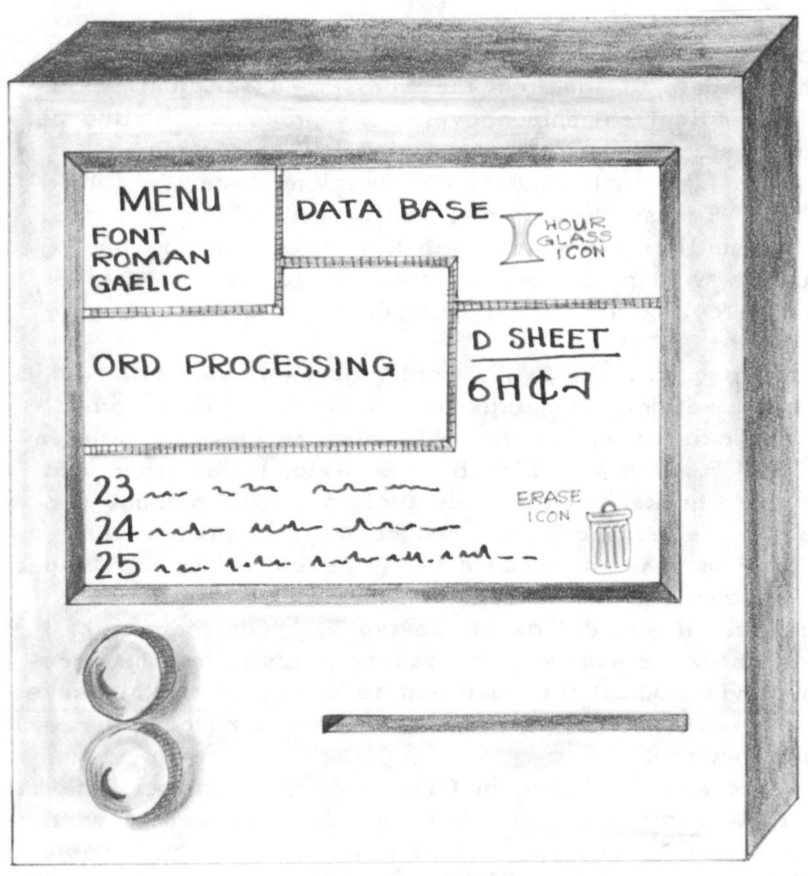

OVERLAPPED WINDOWS

Figure 2.5.2

For example, suppose you wanted to include in a letter, a paragraph from another letter that you had written to your accountant. Instead of having to retype the paragraph into the new letter, the jeweler only has to bring up in the window with the other letter (also called a file), then transfer the paragraph from the old letter to the new letter. Windowing also gives you the ability to go into any other program segment of the I.J.P. and exchange data to and from the word processor, just as in the appraisal example above. This process is called cut-and-paste and can also be called "using a clipboard".

The I.J.P. will include the functions listed in Table 2.5.1. To use these tools, you or your typist will need only familiarize yourself with keystrokes that do the various word processing chores. Table 2.5.1 also gives you a feeling for the jargon used in word processing software.

Along with the I.J.P. word processor, you will have a large electronic thesaurus and dictionary. These programs exist now, but they will play an important role in the I.J.P. You will also have a style, punctuation, and phrase checker. With these tools you will produce perfectly spelled and punctuated documents, write an employee manual and make many professional looking binders all without having to send them to the typesetter and printer. If you did decide to typeset your documents, you can save money by uploading (transferring the document via modem) the document to a typesetter; this saves the typesetter the time of retyping -- or keyboarding -- the document.

As was mentioned in Chapter 4, the Customer Data Base will have all the names and addresses of each of your customers. The I.J.P.'s word processor will be capable of taking data from a Mailing List Data Base and converting it to a format that the word processor will use. We have each received letters that have looked as though they were written personally to us; yet, as we know, it was a form letter that had our name merged into it. These may have contained information that made them seem even more personal. This capacity for a word processor to use a mailing list data base is called mailmerge. For the word processor to be able to use mailmerge, it will have to know where in the document to use the information. The word processor will have a set of codes it assigns to names and addresses. These codes will tell the word processor where to accept the incoming data within the body of the letter. By adjusting spaces, punctuation, and words, the word processor reformats the

Boilerplating features
Capable of using a mouse or light pen
Center text
Change case of letter
Copy Blocked Area To A File
Copy Blocked Area To Cursor
Create Pages Within A Document (Repaginate)
Delete Character On The Left Or Right
Delete To End Of Line
Find And Replace Text (Global Or Singular)
Footer Lines
Go To Previous Page
Go To Top Of Page
Help Screen(S)
HIghlighting
Insert File At Cursor
Insert New Line Boundary
Jump To Bookmark
Justify Paragraph
Macro Key Strokes (Pushing One Key Performs Multiple Functions)
Mail Merge Features
Move Left And Right A Character
Move Left Or Right One Word
Move To Next Tab Stop
Move To Previous Tab Stop
Move Up And Down A Line
Page Combine
Print Document
Print Queue
Push Word Mode
Reformat From Cursor
Save Current File, Switch Files
Scroll Up One Line/Scroll Down One Line
Search Forward Or Backwards For Text
Set Fonts Of Print
Soft Hyphen And Hard Hyphen
Spell Check A File
Strikeover Word Mode
Subscript
Superscript
Transpose With Character On Left Or Right
Windowing

FUNCTIONS OF A WORD PROCESSOR
Table 2.5.1

document to look perfect. Mailmerge features give you a powerful tool for your direct mail advertising campaign. Further, this demonstrates that the more you know about your customers, the more you will personalize your mailings. Such personalization will be an important element of the I.J.P.

Do you need to produce an employee manual or a job description booklet? If you do, you will find the word processor ideal. Once it has been saved on the computer, the manual can be changed and printed whenever necessary. The days will soon be gone when you had to write it out in longhand.

Scientists have developed a machine that will scan printed documents converting the print to American Standard Code for Information Exchange (ASCII code will be used by the Ideal Jewelry Program's word processor). Once available at a reasonable price, you will transfer all your incoming correspondence to the computer's disk storage. This will save on filing space and give a quicker means of access to the correspondence.

Once perfected, this method of information storage, along with laser printers, will dramatically change the way you run your bookkeeping. Any correspondence you receive, you can convert to ASCII, then store that data on the computer's disk storage media. It will then be recalled for use and, as needed, used in other areas of the integrated I.J.P., such as in Appraisals, Correspondence, and Bookkeeping.

Another feature of the Word Processor segment of the Ideal Jewelry Program will be an Outline Processor. What is it? The outline processor is to thinkers as the word processor is to typists. It will free you to organize your thoughts in hierarchical order, with the most important ideas falling in the order you choose. In the Outline Processor, you will be able to suppress the subtopics and only view the main headings or you will be able to see the entire outline.

What benefit does this have for the jeweler? You have to write many letters to customers, employees, colleagues, banks, insurance companies, and so forth. With

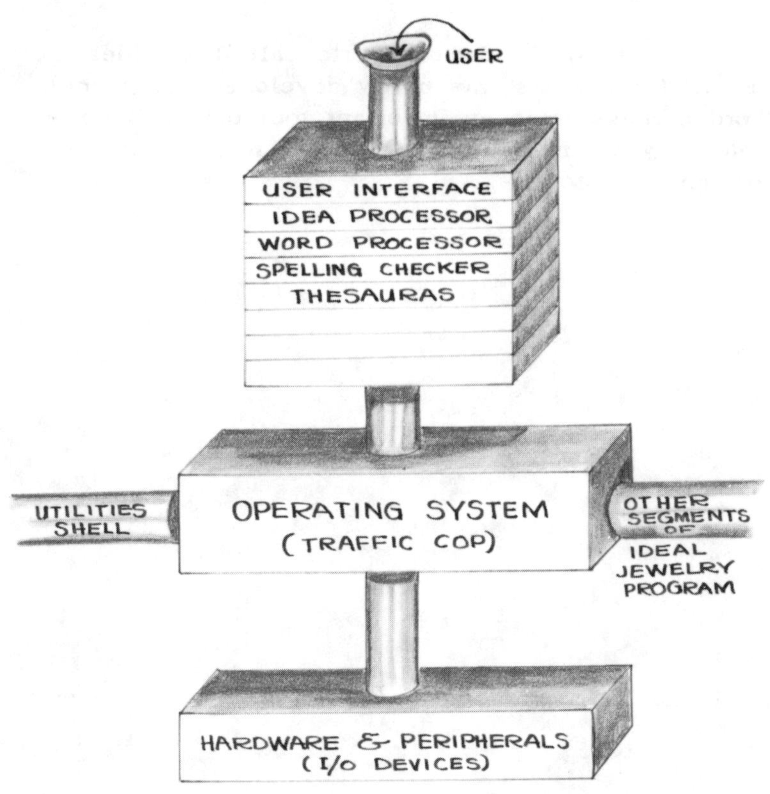

The WORD PROCESSOR IN THE I.J.P.

Figure 2.5.3

the "Outline Processor" you will be able to organize your thoughts in a structured, logical manner. Further, you can produce a daily work list with priorities in descending order. In writing job descriptions it will give you a quicker way of organizing all the tasks under the correct titles.

The most powerful feature of the Outline Processor is that it allows ideas to be seen in ways that will not otherwise be possible. Relationships, nuances, and ideas stand in a new light. Some experts call it an "Idea Processor" (this books was partly developed using one).

Word processing is an important tool that will continue to play an increasingly important role within the modern jewelry store.

6

REPAIR MANAGEMENT AND JOB FLOW

Does the average jewelry store do repairs? Jewelry stores are as varied in the services they offer as they are in their decorum. Some jewelers service jewelry on the premises; others send the jewelry out to be repaired; others don't do it at all. For those who repair on the premises, some have the customer wait; others accept the jewelry for repair and return it within the week. Sometimes, you will repair an item while the customer waits, but will insist the customer make an appointment.

The same applies to appraisals. Not all jewelers have a competent appraiser on staff. They either send out for appraisal services or will have an appraiser come in periodically. The risks you assume when you hold a customer's jewelry for repair and appraisals are high. Further, the manner in which you track the jewelry once it has entered into your store is important. If you do not properly document your outside take-ins, a misplacement will result in embarrassment, both for you and the customer.

If you do a large volume in either appraisals or jewelry repair, the I.J.P. offers a job tracking system that will be of great help to you.

Many customers prefer not to leave jewelry for repair,

but realize the importance of giving you enough time to do the job properly. Some jewelers will give a receipt that has a description of their jewelry as well as the pick-up date for the completion of the jewelry. Other jewelers do not give the customer any documentation.

Whatever method a jeweler follows, the job tracking system will tell you when the job is due, where it will be done, by whom, how much it will cost, how long it will take, what is being repaired, and where the job is right now. At each step in the repair process you will enter the current job status. Of course, each job will be assigned a unique job control number that will be given to the customer: this includes a description of the article of jewelry and the estimated price to complete the repair. The I.J.P. will give you the option of using bar-coded Job Envelopes, which will be discussed in an upcoming chapter. The job tracking system will also show the customer's name, address, and day and evening phone numbers (these will be input into the Customer Data Base and mailing list program).

Once the job has entered the job tracking system, the above data will be available to you at any time. At the completion or transfer of each job to another station (appraisal, special order, and so forth), you will enter the new status. You will have one of your employees fill out a special form that a bookkeeper will enter into the computer later (it is generally most effective to have only one person do data entry).

So that the information will stay valid, each step in the repair of the jewelry should be documented on the computer. Once a job is completed, the computer posted, and the job picked up, you have a plethora of information for use in analyzing your repair business.

For example, you will know how much money your repair and appraisal departments make. You will find out the number of repairs you handle in a week or month, the average price received for each repair, and the average turn around time for repairs and appraisals.

Why is this important? Due to increasing competition for the disposable dollar, you owes it to yourself to make every aspect of your business lucrative. Thus, everything you can do to make your operation more cost effective will obviously be to your advantage. Sometimes

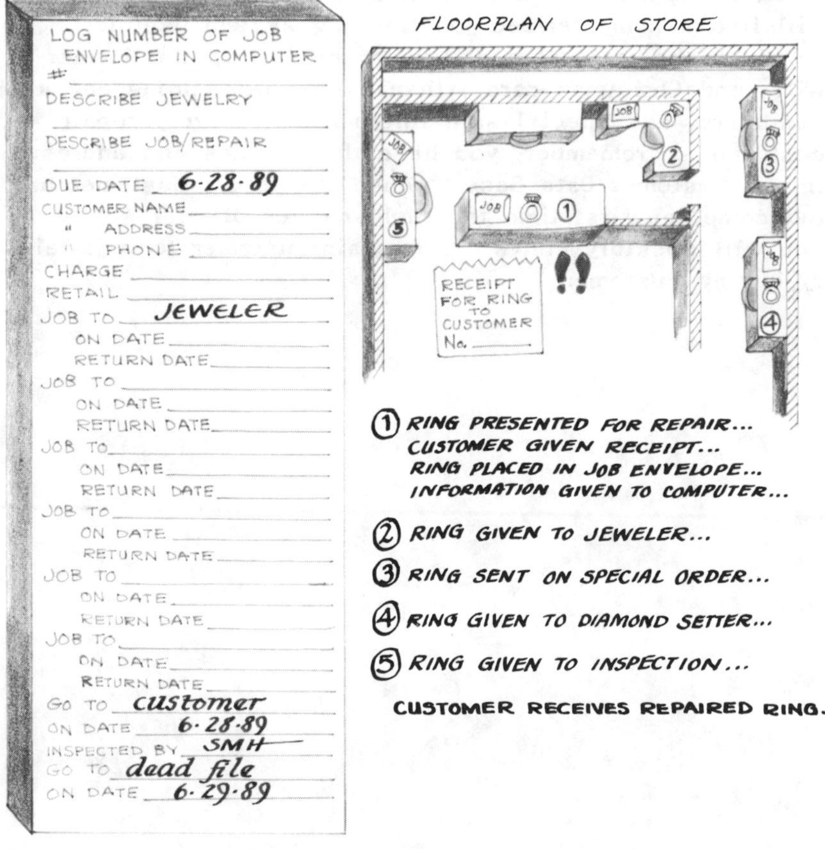

NOTE: After each step in repair job, ring goes back to JOB CONTROL DESK to have status updated on computer before going to next point in the repair process.

JOB CONTROL

Figure 2.6.1

only a few dollars will mean the difference between profit and loss. Some jewelers are not large enough to benefit from the computerized job tracking system, but those doing over $400,000 per year with greater than 10% of this revenue coming from the repair and appraisals department will find a computerized job tracking system useful.

Given the integrated nature of the I.J.P., the jeweler will send Christmas cards, thank you notes, prong check-up reminders, and special sale information to every repair customer -- remember, you have their names and addresses in the Customer Data Base. Since the repair customer has overcome the first-time threshold barrier of your store, you will possibly convert the repair customer to a jewelry-buying customer.

7

THE ADVANTAGES OF AN ELECTRONIC SPREADSHEET

DISCUSSION OF TERMS

TEMPLATE--A mathematical model of a business that uses a spreadsheet program as the basis of its creation.

Why are electronic spreadsheets so popular? A Spreadsheet is an electronic number manipulator. Cells of numbers and formulas can be entered on a template. The cells are tied together with other cells so that a change in one will affect another. Built in functions such as date and time functions, sum of row or columns, sine and cosine, and many other useful business and scientific formulas can be input into a template (see table 2.7.2). The more memory the computer has, the larger the model can be. Once a series of interrelated cells of formulas and numbers have been input into the Spreadsheet, you will be able to automatically recompute the entire model by the stroke of one or two buttons. If you wanted to see what effect one change will have on the rest of the model, the Spreadsheet will automatically recompute the entire template, giving you the reach to do financial "What-If" analysis.

Because accountants and businessmen used to do "What-If" analysis by hand -- a lengthy process, the electronic Spreadsheet has become popular. Electronic Spreadsheets, the programs that made microcomputers as popular as they are today, are a significant business analysis tool for you. In depth financial models of your business will be created by using Spreadsheet templates (a template is a mathematical model of a business that uses a Spreadsheet program as its foundation). The latest electronic spreadsheets include sophisticated data base features that offer a quick means of finding and sorting data (see Table 2.7.1). Spreadsheet programs include business graphics capabilities that enable you to create charts and graphs that at a glance will depict the status of your business.

Table 2.7.3 gives the graphics capabilities of a good Spreadsheet program. These graphics capabilities will be used to get a graphic representation of your business: this will include a monthly comparison of sales per salesperson compared over the last 3 years. Posting this graph in an employee area will give the employees a benchmark of their sales performance and will challenge them to better their past year's performance.

You can devise a template that automatically recomputes the current retail and wholesale diamond prices of all diamonds in stock. Each diamond is tied together via color, clarity, shape, and size to a cell that has the current wholesale price per carat for that particular diamond. At a moment's notice, you will find the current value of your diamonds at cost and retail. You will also determine the average price and weight of diamonds that you had in stock. Although the Inventory Control segment of the I.J.P. will do this too, it does show you the individual power and flexibility of the Electronic Spreadsheet, when used alone.

COPY
DATA
DATA QUERY
DATA QUERY CRITERION
DATA QUERY DELETE
DATA QUERY EXTRACT
DATA QUERY FIND
DATA SORT
DATA TABLE
DATA TABLE RESET
DELETE ROW
FILE SAVE
FILE EXTRACT FORMULAS
GRAPH
GRAPH OPTIONS
MOVE
PRINT FILE
PRINT PRINTER
RANGE ERASE
RANGE FORMAT
RANGE FORMAT DATE
RANGE NAME
RANGE NAME CREATE
WORKSHEET COLUMN SET
WORKSHEET GLOBAL FORMAT
WORKSHEET GLOBAL RECALCULATION ITERATIVE
WORKSHEET GLOBAL RECALCULATION MANUAL
WORKSHEET INSERT COLUMN
WORKSHEET INSERT ROW
WORKSHEET WINDOW HORIZONTAL
WORKSHEET WINDOW VERTICAL

SPREADSHEET COMMANDS

Table 2.7.1

ABSOLUTE VALUE
ARC TANGENT
AVERAGE VALUE
BOOLEAN LOGIC
- AND
- IF
- OR

CHOOSE FUNCTION
COUNT
DATE AND DAY FUNCTIONS
ERROR VALUE
INTEGER FUNCTIONS
LOG
LOOKUP FUNCTIONS
MAXIMUM AND MINIMUM VALUES
MODULO FUNCTION
MONTH FUNCTION
NATURAL NUMBER
NET PRESENT VALUE
PAYMENT VALUE
PRESENT VALUE
ROUND FUNCTION
SINE AND COSINE
SQUARE ROOT
STANDARD DEVIATION
SUM VALUE
VARIANCE

SPREADSHEET FUNCTIONS

Table 2.7.2

AREA AND HI LO CHARTS
AUTOMATIC SCALE SETTINGS
BAR CHARTS
CROSS HATCHING OF CHARTS
COLOR LEGEND
TITLES
FORMATTING
LEGENDS
SYMBOLS
PIE CHARTS
REGRESSION LINE
SCALE OPTIONS
SCATTER PLOTS
SHADING PATTERNS
SIMPLE BAR CHART
STACKED BAR CHART
SUBTITLES
TITLES

SPREADSHEET GRAPHICS

Table 2.7.3

The employee work schedule will also be simple to do on a spreadsheet. Assigning a series of cells to an employee, you will see how many hours have been assigned every week, every two weeks, and every month. By adding up all the employees's hours, you will keep track of total employee hours, total part-time hours, the ratio of part-time hours to full-time hours, and the ratio of part and full-time hours to total hours. This helps to more closely control labor costs. It will be clear if too many or too few employees were scheduled during certain key hours of the day. This template, once set into operation, will save half the time it will normally take to prepare a schedule.

In the I.J.P., the Spreadsheet will be able to do all the above and more. Its functions will be integrated with the other portions of the program, providing the ability to analyze payroll, accounts receivable, accounts payable, the general ledger, and the Customer Data Base. Also it will be closely integrated with the word processor and the graphics part of the program.

Another area in which a Spreadsheet will prove useful is open-to-buys. Here you will have much closer control over your inventory spending. Again, you will play "What-If:" what if I spend less money with this vendor and put more money into that one? How will this effect the complete financial picture? Once I have spent my money on this vendor, how much will that leave me for the remaining season? How does this compare to what I spent last year? What will I have to sell this month to stay on schedule? If I overspend, where will I have to cut back? The Spreadsheet is ideal for maintaining your open-to-buys.

Table 2.7.4 is a list of other areas in which you will find the Spreadsheet a valuable tool.

You can develop a template that will examine your payroll and compare it to your gross sales. For instance, should your net profit drop and your salary increase to greater than 24% of your gross sales, you will be heading for trouble. By looking at other key indicators, you will know at a glance your business's health. Accountants call this technique ratio analysis, and your understanding of ratio analysis will be a major step towards keeping your business healthy. Before making any decisions that will affect your bottom line, you should input the effect of these decisions into your financial models.

Store Schedule

Date: 9MAR to 22Mar89

NAMES		FRIDAY 9TH	SATURDAY 10TH	SUNDAY 11TH	MONDAY 12TH	TUESDAY 13TH	WEDNESDAY 14TH	THURS 15TH	TOTAL HRS
PETE	M	2.5			2.5		2.5	2.5	
	A	4.5	OFF	OFF	4.5	OFF	4.5	4.5	28.0
	E								
TOM	M		1.011		2.5	2.5			
	A	5.5	5.5	OFF	5.5	5.5	OFF	3.52	42.0
	E	3.5	3.5					3.5	
PHILL	M							2.5	
	A	5.5	OFF	OFF	5.5	5.5	3.52	5.5	42.0
	E	3.5			3.5	3.5	3.5		
MARY	M	2.5	2.5		1				
	A	5	4	[illegible].5		5.5	5.5	OFF	40.5
	E					3.5	3.5		
KIM	M								
	A		1.54	5.5		OFF	OFF	4.51	25.6
	E	3.5	3.5		3.5			3.5	
TINA	M	2.5			2.5	2.5	2.5	2.5	
	A	3.5	OFF	OFF	3.5	5.5	2.5	3	30.5
	E								
SID	M		2.5			2.5	2.5		
	A	OFF	4	OFF			4	2.53	25.0
	E				3.5			3.5	
RENE	M								
	A		5.5	5.012	OFF		0.55	OFF	25.1
	E	3.5	3.5			3.5	3.5		
MORN=2.5H		3	2	0	3	3	3	3	
AFTE=5.5H		4	4	3	3	4	4	4	258.7
EVEN=3.5H		4	3	0	3	3	3	3	

MORN=9:30-1200 %PART-TIME TO HOURS = 42.5%
AFTE=12-5:30 TOTAL PART TIME HRS = 221.84
EVEN=5:30-9:00

Mary's hours... taken from chart...

SPREADSHEET OF EMPLOYEE HOURS

Figure 2.7.4a

Store Schedule

FRIDAY 16TH	SATURDAY 17TH	SUNDAY 18TH	MONDAY 19TH	TUESDAY 20TH	WEDNESDAY 21ST	THURS 22ND	TOTAL HRS
2.5 4.5	OFF	OFF	2.5 4.5	OFF	2.5 4.5	2.5 4.5	28.0
4.51 3.5	2.5 4.5	OFF	5.5 3.5	2.5 5.5	OFF	5.5 3.5	41.0
OFF	5.5 3.5	6.5	5.5 3.5	OFF	3.52 3.5	5.5 3.5	40.5
2.5 3.5	2.5 5.5	7.5	OFF	3.52 3.5	2.5 1.5	1.54 3.5	37.6
3.5	0.55 3.5	5.5	OFF	0.55 3.5	2.033 3.5	OFF	22.6
2.5 5.5	OFF	OFF	2.5 3	2.5 4.5	2.5 5.5	2.5 3.5	34.5
2.5 5.5	2.5 2	OFF	2.5 4.5	2.5 5.5	OFF	3.5	31.0
3.5	3.52 3.5	OFF	3.5	3.5	1.54 3.5	2.5 2.5	27.6
4 4 3	3 4 3	0 4 0	3 4 3	3 4 3	3 3 3	3 4 4	262.8

Figure 2.7.4b

Calculating Growth Capacity
Determining the Cost of Opportunity in
    Carrying Inventory Over Fixed Time
    Periods
Fixed Asset Management
Lease vs Debt Financing
Loan Amortization
Managing Cash Flow
Performing RATIO ANALYSIS
  including:
    Balance Sheet and Income
      Statement Ratios
    Liquidity Indicators
    Profitability Ratios
    Solvency Indicators
Projecting Cash Flow
Tracking a Line of Credit

ADDITIONAL USES
FOR
AN ELECTRONIC SPREADSHEET

Table 2.7.4

Electronic Spreadsheets give you the power to analyze your financial posture today. Remember that all the segments of the I.J.P. are integrated; you will be able to tie columns of figures, charts, and complex graphs together with your word processor. Should you want to expand your business, you will sway your loan institute with your professional business acumen. Coupled with the other segments of the Ideal Jewelry Program, the Electronic Spreadsheet will be one more reason the you might not want to be without a computer.

Electronic Spreadsheet

```
                THE EMPLOYEE HOURLY ANALYSIS REPORT
                               FOR
                     THE IDEAL JEWELRY STORE
=========================================================================
Number of Employees currently employeed:     PUT IN AMT HERE ||        3
==================================WORKSHEET==============================
List all employee's job titles and hours each works per week:
-------------------------------------------------------------------------
TITLES:                                   || BOOKKEEPER 1 =====>        0
OWNER==============>                   62 || BOOKKEEPER 2 =====>        0
GENERAL MANAGER====>                   53 || CASHIER ==========>       43
MANAGER============>                    0 ||=============================
ASSISTANT MANAGER==>                    0 || TOTAL HOURS              158
APPRAISER==========>                    0 || TOTAL PART TIME HOURS      0
SALESPERSON 1======>                    0 || % OF PART TIME TO FULL   0.0
SALESPERSON 2======>                    0 || OVERTIME HOURS             3
SALESPERSON 3======>                    0 || % OVERTIME TO REGULAR   1.90
SALSEPERSON 4======>                    0 || TOTAL PAYROLL        1048.00
SALESPERSON 5======>                    0 || % PAYROLL TO GROSS SALES 17.5
=====================================||==================================
```

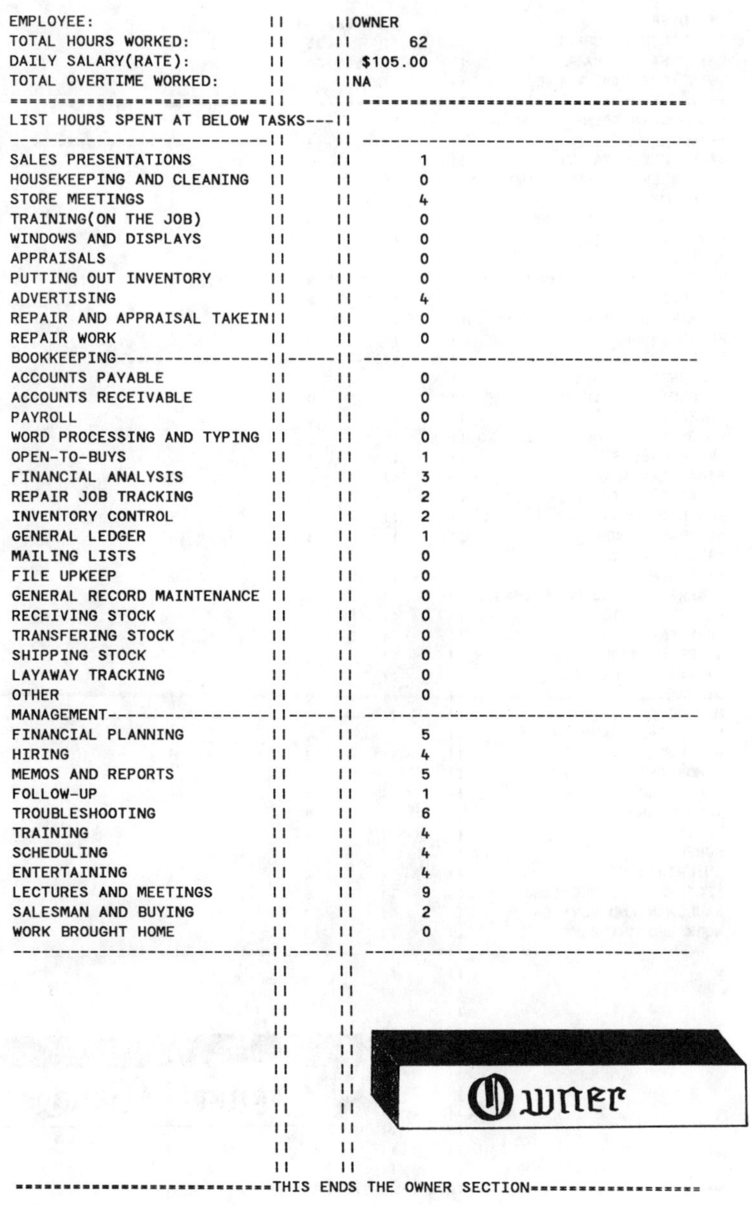

```
EMPLOYEE:                    ||     ||OWNER
TOTAL HOURS WORKED:          ||     ||      62
DAILY SALARY(RATE):          ||     || $105.00
TOTAL OVERTIME WORKED:       ||     ||NA
===========================||     || ================================
LIST HOURS SPENT AT BELOW TASKS---||
---------------------------||     || ----------------------------------
SALES PRESENTATIONS          ||     ||       1
HOUSEKEEPING AND CLEANING    ||     ||       0
STORE MEETINGS               ||     ||       4
TRAINING(ON THE JOB)         ||     ||       0
WINDOWS AND DISPLAYS         ||     ||       0
APPRAISALS                   ||     ||       0
PUTTING OUT INVENTORY        ||     ||       0
ADVERTISING                  ||     ||       4
REPAIR AND APPRAISAL TAKEIN||     ||       0
REPAIR WORK                  ||     ||       0
BOOKKEEPING-----------------||-----|| ----------------------------------
ACCOUNTS PAYABLE             ||     ||       0
ACCOUNTS RECEIVABLE          ||     ||       0
PAYROLL                      ||     ||       0
WORD PROCESSING AND TYPING   ||     ||       0
OPEN-TO-BUYS                 ||     ||       1
FINANCIAL ANALYSIS           ||     ||       3
REPAIR JOB TRACKING          ||     ||       2
INVENTORY CONTROL            ||     ||       2
GENERAL LEDGER               ||     ||       1
MAILING LISTS                ||     ||       0
FILE UPKEEP                  ||     ||       0
GENERAL RECORD MAINTENANCE   ||     ||       0
RECEIVING STOCK              ||     ||       0
TRANSFERING STOCK            ||     ||       0
SHIPPING STOCK               ||     ||       0
LAYAWAY TRACKING             ||     ||       0
OTHER                        ||     ||       0
MANAGEMENT------------------||-----|| ----------------------------------
FINANCIAL PLANNING           ||     ||       5
HIRING                       ||     ||       4
MEMOS AND REPORTS            ||     ||       5
FOLLOW-UP                    ||     ||       1
TROUBLESHOOTING              ||     ||       6
TRAINING                     ||     ||       4
SCHEDULING                   ||     ||       4
ENTERTAINING                 ||     ||       4
LECTURES AND MEETINGS        ||     ||       9
SALESMAN AND BUYING          ||     ||       2
WORK BROUGHT HOME            ||     ||       0
---------------------------||-----|| ---------------------------------
                             ||     ||
                             ||     ||
                             ||     ||
                             ||     ||
                             ||     ||
                             ||     ||
                             ||     ||
                             ||     ||
                             ||     ||
                             ||     ||
=========================THIS ENDS THE OWNER SECTION=================
```


Figure 2.7.6b

EMPLOYEE:	GENERAL MANAGER
TOTAL HOURS WORKED:	53
DAILY SALARY(RATE):	$95.00
TOTAL OVERTIME WORKED:	NA
LIST HOURS SPENT AT BELOW TASKS---	
SALES PRESENTATIONS	0
HOUSEKEEPING AND CLEANING	0
STORE MEETINGS	7
TRAINING(ON THE JOB)	0
WINDOWS AND DISPLAYS	0
APPRAISALS	0
PUTTING OUT INVENTORY	0
ADVERTISING	2
REPAIR AND APPRAISAL TAKEIN	0
REPAIR WORK	0
BOOKKEEPING---	
ACCOUNTS PAYABLE	0
ACCOUNTS RECEIVABLE	0
PAYROLL	0
WORD PROCESSING AND TYPING	0
OPEN-TO-BUYS	3
FINANCIAL ANALYSIS	2
REPAIR JOB TRACKING	1
INVENTORY CONTROL	2
GENERAL LEDGER	1
MAILING LISTS	0
FILE UPKEEP	0
GENERAL RECORD MAINTENANCE	0
RECEIVING STOCK	0
TRANSFERING STOCK	0
SHIPPING STOCK	0
LAYAWAY TRACKING	0
OTHER	0
MANAGEMENT---	
FINANCIAL PLANNING	4
HIRING	3
MEMOS AND REPORTS	3
FOLLOW-UP	1
TROUBLESHOOTING	6
TRAINING	4
SCHEDULING	4
ENTERTAINING	2
LECTURES AND MEETINGS	6
SALESMAN AND BUYING	2
WORK BROUGHT HOME	0

General Manager

=====THIS ENDS THE GENERAL MANAGER SECTION=====

Figure 2.7.6c

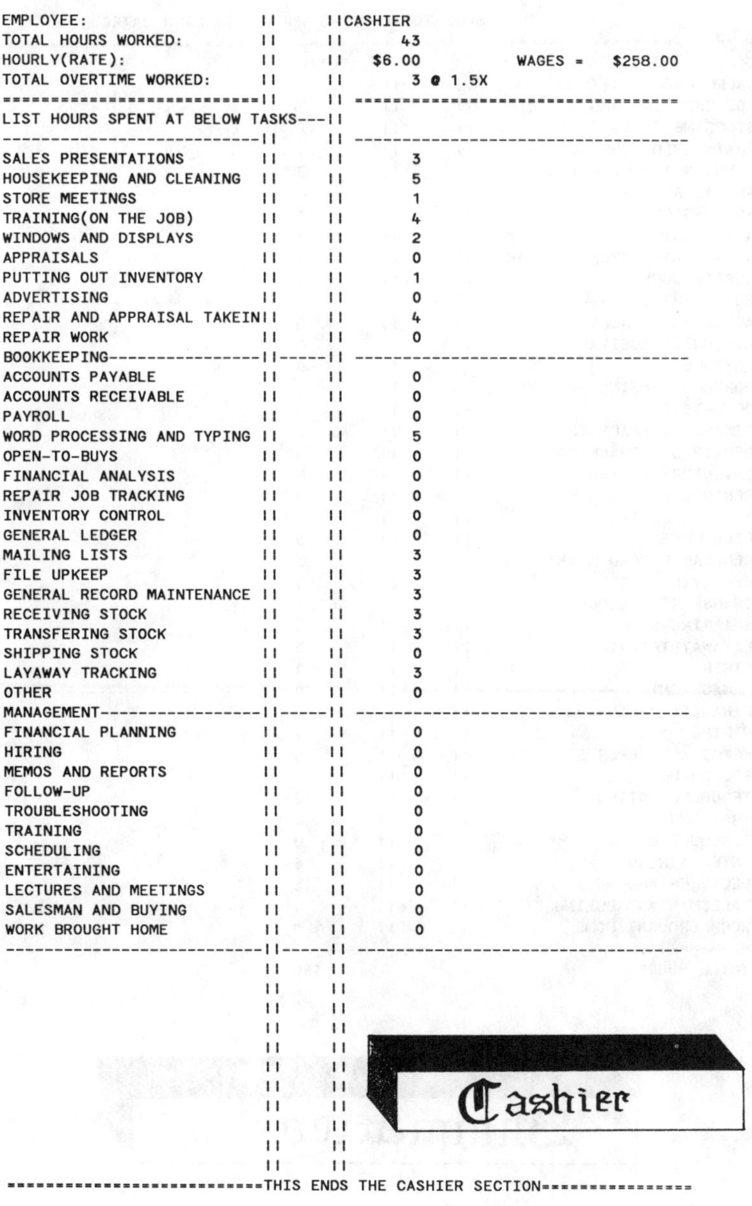

```
EMPLOYEE:                   ||      ||CASHIER
TOTAL HOURS WORKED:         ||      ||      43
HOURLY(RATE):               ||      ||   $6.00          WAGES =    $258.00
TOTAL OVERTIME WORKED:      ||      ||       3 @ 1.5X
===========================||      || ==================================
LIST HOURS SPENT AT BELOW TASKS---||
---------------------------||      || -----------------------------------
SALES PRESENTATIONS         ||      ||       3
HOUSEKEEPING AND CLEANING   ||      ||       5
STORE MEETINGS              ||      ||       1
TRAINING(ON THE JOB)        ||      ||       4
WINDOWS AND DISPLAYS        ||      ||       2
APPRAISALS                  ||      ||       0
PUTTING OUT INVENTORY       ||      ||       1
ADVERTISING                 ||      ||       0
REPAIR AND APPRAISAL TAKEIN||      ||       4
REPAIR WORK                 ||      ||       0
BOOKKEEPING-----------------||-----|| -----------------------------------
ACCOUNTS PAYABLE            ||      ||       0
ACCOUNTS RECEIVABLE         ||      ||       0
PAYROLL                     ||      ||       0
WORD PROCESSING AND TYPING  ||      ||       5
OPEN-TO-BUYS                ||      ||       0
FINANCIAL ANALYSIS          ||      ||       0
REPAIR JOB TRACKING         ||      ||       0
INVENTORY CONTROL           ||      ||       0
GENERAL LEDGER              ||      ||       0
MAILING LISTS               ||      ||       3
FILE UPKEEP                 ||      ||       3
GENERAL RECORD MAINTENANCE  ||      ||       3
RECEIVING STOCK             ||      ||       3
TRANSFERING STOCK           ||      ||       3
SHIPPING STOCK              ||      ||       0
LAYAWAY TRACKING            ||      ||       3
OTHER                       ||      ||       0
MANAGEMENT------------------||-----|| -----------------------------------
FINANCIAL PLANNING          ||      ||       0
HIRING                      ||      ||       0
MEMOS AND REPORTS           ||      ||       0
FOLLOW-UP                   ||      ||       0
TROUBLESHOOTING             ||      ||       0
TRAINING                    ||      ||       0
SCHEDULING                  ||      ||       0
ENTERTAINING                ||      ||       0
LECTURES AND MEETINGS       ||      ||       0
SALESMAN AND BUYING         ||      ||       0
WORK BROUGHT HOME           ||      ||       0
---------------------------||-----|| ----------------------------------
                            ||      ||
                            ||      ||
                            ||      ||
                            ||      ||
                            ||      ||
                            ||      ||
                            ||      ||
                            ||      ||
                            ||      ||
                            ||      ||
                            ||      ||
==========================THIS ENDS THE CASHIER SECTION===============
```


Figure 2.7.6d

THIS SUMS TOTAL HOURS WORKED IN EACH CATEGORY

JOBS			TOTAL
SALES PRESENTATIONS			4
HOUSEKEEPING AND CLEANING			5
STORE MEETINGS			12
TRAINING(ON THE JOB)			4
WINDOWS AND DISPLAYS			2
APPRAISALS			0
PUTTING OUT INVENTORY			1
ADVERTISING			6
REPAIR AND APPRAISAL TAKEIN			4
REPAIR WORK			0
BOOKKEEPING			0
ACCOUNTS PAYABLE			0
ACCOUNTS RECEIVABLE			0
PAYROLL			0
WORD PROCESSING AND TYPING			5
OPEN-TO-BUYS			4
FINANCIAL ANALYSIS			5
REPAIR JOB TRACKING			3
INVENTORY CONTROL			4
GENERAL LEDGER			2
MAILING LISTS			3
FILE UPKEEP			3
GENERAL RECORD MAINTENANCE			3
RECEIVING STOCK			3
TRANSFERING STOCK			3
SHIPPING STOCK			0
LAYAWAY TRACKING			3
OTHER			0
MANAGEMENT			0
FINANCIAL PLANNING			9
HIRING			7
MEMOS AND REPORTS			8
FOLLOW-UP			2
TROUBLESHOOTING			12
TRAINING			8
SCHEDULING			8
ENTERTAINING			6
LECTURES AND MEETINGS			15
SALESMAN AND BUYING			4
WORK BROUGHT HOME			0
TOTAL HOURS	=		158

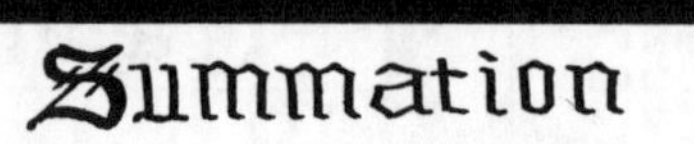

Figure 2.7.6e

8

INVENTORY CONTROL (IC)

DISCUSSION OF TERMS

BAR CODE--Marking products using bars of different thicknesses to represent numbers and characters, such as (UPC) Universal Product Codes, 3 of 9, Codabar, and others.

CODABAR--A code system using special symbols and numbers, it is used by the Library of Congress, on blood bags and photo finishing bags,etc.

CODE 39--An alpha-numeric bar code that can be read in two directions with a bar code scanner and can vary in length. "3 of 9" means each character is nine elements, three of which will be wide.

COST-OF-OPPORTUNITY--When inventory is not turning over quickly enough, the cost-of-opportunity is the money spent on overhead, employees, and inventory that could have been earning interest in a bank. In other words, by reducing inventory levels while maintaining stock turn and markup gives the jeweler added cash and therefore profit. Imagine earning interest on this extra cash instead of putting it in slow moving merchandise. Some experts claim the cost-of-opportunity for the jeweler is equal to approximately 20 to 25% of his annual average inventory per year. That means that if he were to reduce his inventory by 25% and still meet his selling quotas, he will make 1/4 of 25% of his inventory in extra profit and in addition have that extra 25%, not spent on inventory, in dollars to spend as needed in the business.

DATA ENTRY--The process of entering data into a computer.

HISTORICAL DATA--Past sales records on an item in inventory. Historical data can be reviewed to determine the salability and stocking position of individual items of jewelry.

JULIAN DATE--A four digit code in which the first digit stands for the last digit of the current year, the last three digits stand for the number of days since the first day of the year. An example follows: 6030 or January 30, 1986. In reality this could be any decade but in business uses, most people will be able to relate the julian date with the current decade.

LEAD TIME--The time it takes to order and receive an item. Different items will have different lead times. These can be determined and this information used to assist the jeweler in placing orders for merchandise.

NO-HIT--Merchandise that has not sold. Being able to identify these items can lead to greater stock turn and sale of these items.

NON-SIM--Classification for an item that sells only once in six months. It stands for Non-Special Inventory Item Management. A SIM item will convert to Non-SIM if after 6 months it is not hit one or more times. The U.S. Navy uses this method in its inventory management programs.

PERPETUAL INVENTORY--This term is used to describe an inventory system in which the jeweler will know at all times what his on hand balance of any stock item. He will know how many are on order, how many have been received, and how many have been sold.

POINT-OF-SALE(POS)--Electronic means of automating inventory control using cash register as means of input. The process can be further simplified by the use of bar codes for stock entry information.

RANGE--Number of different styles of jewelry stocked.

SCANNER--A portable unit used to identify and hold coded information that can later by transferred to a computer such as in a bar code scanner.

SPECIAL INVENTORY MANAGEMENT(SIM)--Classification for merchandise that sells rapidly-twice in six months. It stands for Selected Item Management. This designation is used by the U.S. Navy in its inventory management systems. By designating jewelry as SIM and Non-SIM allows jewelers to more closely control hot selling items. A SIM program is nothing more than determining what sells and watching these on a routine basis.

SPIFF-Bonus paid to a salesperson for selling a particular piece of jewelry. Often used to create interest in selling slow-moving items.

STOCK OUT--Situation of low merchandise supply and high traffic of customers resulting in loss of business. This could result from attempts to lower inventory investment to such a degree that sales are lost owing to a lack of proper inventory.

STOCK TURN--Term used to indicate the amount of times that merchandise sells in a given period of time. One popular formula is

$$\frac{\text{sales at cost}}{\text{average inventory at cost}}$$

VALIDITY--The degree of accuracy found in inventory records when compared to the actual on-hand count of merchandise. As time passes between storewide (wall-to-wall) inventories the validity of stock records decrease. To restore inventory to a higher validity an inventory either partial or full, should be taken.

WAND--Pen-like device used to transfer bar code information to a bar code scanner.

Ideally, you want to sell every piece of jewelry you have at least once, if not more, per year. If you can always keep enough fast-moving jewelry in stock and yet never have too much that you can't sell it quickly, you will be in jeweler's heaven.

The game is to sell more often what you do have, and the more the better. If merchandise sits too long, the money tied up in insurance, maintenance, rent, and employees will have been better saved, and the money used to first buy the merchandise better sent to the bank. The money lost by not having it in the bank is called the cost-of-opportunity. The term that means to sell more jewelry, more times, more often is called stock turn. Naturally, you, like other retailers, need a basic supply of products in order to maintain a given volume of business. If the products aren't there but the customers are, you have lost business caused by stock out. If the customer's aren't there and the products are there, you have a lack of traffic. But, if the customers are there and the product is there in equal balance -- you have proper Inventory Control procedures. The Inventory Control (IC) segment will give you the tools with which you can create this balance.

High value items mirror most of your inventory. For

virtually all jewelers, the range (different styles) of jewelry is broad, the depth (the number of one style stocked) is narrow. The average stock turn of jewelry is, on the average, low -- usually around 1 turn per year. Automating the IC process will give you greater control over your inventory. You will track fast moving items, insuring a steady supply is available; and you will track slow moving jewelry, insuring action is taken to create interest in them such as by offering spiffs (a bonus to the salesperson who sells it) or discounts.

The IC Segment will be a perpetual inventory system. Perpetual holds that, with reasonable record keeping accuracy, records will reflect, at any given time, the actual on-hand inventory. IC records will show on-order and on-hand balances, gains and losses, and returns and transfers. With a perpetual inventory system, you will have to take fewer wall-to-wall inventories; you will concentrate on departmental inventories in which you count the stock of one department at a time. By spreading these inventories out over the year, you will maintain a high stock validity (the degree to which stock records reflect actual counts of on-hand stock) and at the same time spot trouble areas in which greater controls may need to be taken.

In general, if one style of ring sells twice in one year (called a two time stock turn) you should not be long without it; if the ring sells twice in six months, you should not be without it and should have another on order; if the ring sells twice in 3 months, you should not be without 2 of the same ring. If the lead time (time it takes to order and receive a ring from the manufacturer) for a ring is 6 weeks, you should plan your reorder based on this. To track lead times, each vendor will be assigned a lead time code. The Ideal Jewelry Program's IC segment will provide reports of all items that have sold. It will give those styles that have sold once, twice, three, four, and more times quarterly, semiannually, and annually; the Economic Order Quantity section of the IC segment will provide this information.

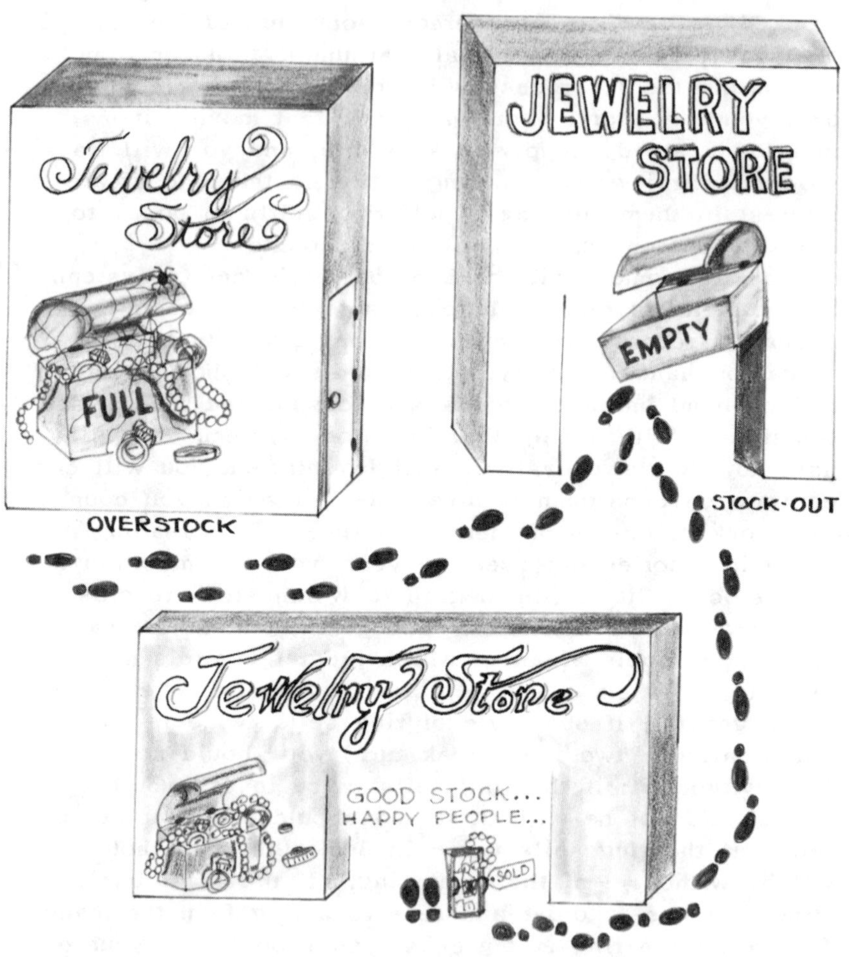

PROPER INVENTORY CONTROL

Figure 2.8.1

PERPETUAL INVENTORY

Jewelry on hand = Beginning Balance + Receipts − Expenditures

PERPETUAL INVENTORY

Figure 2.8.2

Unique to the clothing and jewelry industry is the role fashion plays in the stocking of merchandise. After you attend regional jewelry shows, you have fresh new styles you wants to try, but have no historical data (past sales records for the item) on these new styles -- only a gut feeling that they will sell. Having ordered five new rings, one sells within the first week, one sits for two years, the rest sell within the first year -- why? Inventory Control is an art and a science: the better you understand your business, clients, merchandise, and I.J.P., the better you will be able to make educated choices about your inventory purchases.

Sound IC procedures apply to your inventory as much as they apply to any business. Jewelry that sells needs special attention. The United States Navy calls this -- Special Item Management (SIM). If an item sells twice in six months, they call it a SIM item. If it sells less than twice within 6 months, it is a NON-SIM item. If it is a SIM item, but after an additional 6 months doesn't sell again, they convert it to a NON-SIM. Initially all stock is called a NO HIT -- it saw no action. Once sold, it becomes a NON-SIM.

The IC segment will show you your customer's buying habits during the changing seasons. Some items will sell better during certain periods of the year, others will sell well all year. In the spring, to order the items that sell in the fall, or to stock jewelry that your clients will be unlikely to buy, is imprudent buying. You will let the inventory dollars work for you by buying the right stock at the right time. Without an I.J.P. you cannot expect to fully follow the trends; with the I.J.P.'s IC segment, you will closely watch your SIM items, increase your stock turn, and bank more money. The I.J.P. will make it easy for you to follow trends; it will give you the tools you need to buy wisely.

Creative promotions play an important role in increasing stock turn. For example, imagine the cocktail ring department has a turnover rate of 1.0, called a one-time turnover -- or stock turn.

To create greater stock turn, you can advertise cocktail rings, you can create enthusiasm about cocktail rings among your employees, and you can hold special sales on cocktail rings. The most profitable way to increase turnover will be to choose a method that does not sacrifice price for turnover. If you will manage to increase turnover by 50% and maintain your markup, your profit will increase by 50%, minus the cost of the promotion.

The I.J.P.'s IC segment will make it easy for you to understand your profit centers, your markup, your turnover, your SIM and NON-SIM items. The segment will make it easier, faster and less expensive for you to order, tag, check, and receive jewelry. Further, the I.J.P. gives the choice to be Point-of-Sale (POS) or non-POS.

Table 2.8.1 lists the major features of the IC segment.

ANNUAL TURNOVER=
Annual cost of goods sold/
Average inventory

MONTHLY TURNOVER ON INDIVIDUAL ITEM=
Number of items sold year-to-date/Average number of same item sold per month

TURNOVER

Figure 2.8.3

Point of Sale (POS)
Receiving and Marking Merchandise Control
Ease of Sales Entry
Merchandise Aging
Ease of Taking Physical Inventories
Automatic Replenishment of SIM ITEMS
Layaway Tracking
Pricing of Inventory Using Different Levels (ie. gold, diamonds, others)
Print Standard and Bar Code Tags
Allows use of LIFO, FIFO, or Inventory Averaging
Monitors Inventory Shrinkage
Reports Inventory Overages and Shortages
Provides for Departmental Management
Has Three Tiered Security access
Provides Economic Order Quantities Analysis
Customized to the Jeweler's Business

INVENTORY CONTROL SEGMENT

Table 2.8.1

LAYAWAY TRACKING

Layaways help you close more sales. If the customer is unable to use credit or cash, the layaway sale may be the only way for him to purchase the merchandise. For most jewelry stores, layaway policies vary. Some jewelers allow layaways of up to a year; others, three months. During the time in which items are on layaway, the merchandise is out of circulation. As a result, layaways will represent a substantial reduction in working inventory. Thus, an easy method of monitoring, reviewing, and purging your layaways will be in the jeweler's best interest. The IC segment allows you to do just that.

Within the layaway tracking section of the IC segment, you will be provided with status and data about layaways. This section will tell you which layaways were beyond the time limit and which had not been paid recently. It will tell you the total dollar value at cost and retail in layaway and will recommend which layaways should be returned to stock.

LEVELS OF PRICING

In the I.J.P., you will establish a standard markup for different price ranges of inventory. Once done, the program will automatically compute inventory values based on these markups. If you desired to change one group of inventory, the IC segment will give you the flexibility to do so. The program will also provide you with the means to price stock at various levels of cost and retail (for example, the special promotional pricing mentioned earlier).

The IC segment will also give you access to the di amond catalogue discussed in Chapter 14. This will be, in effect, a sub-segment of the IC segment. Here you will be able to maintain updated prices on diamonds, and see where your diamond inventory is in relation to your cost versus its current market value. It will give you statistics regarding the diamonds, including total value -- cost and retail, average mark up, total weight of di amonds, average weight, average color and clarity, mis sing color and clarity grades in a preestablished inven tory wish list. For example, you want to always have fifths, quarters, and halves in 4 quality levels, ie. VVS1, G; SI1, E; SI2, J; and VS1, G in stock, but if the program detected one of these categories was missing, it will signal you so that you can order it.

Because many of your appraisals consist of jewelry purchased at your store, the Appraisal segment of the I.J.P. will have a direct link to the IC segment. You will then be able to join descriptions and prices of jewelry in the IC segment with information in the Appraisal segment.

POINT-OF-SALE (POS)

POS is the electronic means of automating IC using the cash register as the main means of input. POS will include Electronic Funds Transfer Systems (EFTS). A POS with EFTS will include an automatic means of controlling inventory at the cash register and will include credit authorization, credit verification, and Electronic Fund Transfers (EFTS) at the POS terminal.

Not all jewelers will need a POS system, while others will need only parts of one. These systems usually are cost effective in large retail outlets that have a high rate of sales (such as grocery stores). The major advantages of POS are that sales data are only entered once (meaning less errors) and customers are thus handled more efficiently. POS also updates the Inventory, at the same time creating a receipt for the customer. It provides up-to-the-minute information regarding on-hand stock balances. Two problems to solve are its high cost of implementation and the difficulty of putting bar coded stock tags on small jewelry tags (the bar code readers find them more difficult to read).

In the I.J.P. the cost of implementing a POS will be greatly reduced and the tag problem will be solved. The bar codes and the bar code reading machines will then be the common data entry convention used in POS. Figure 2.8.4 shows the common features of the POS cash register.

Today. you sell jewelry, write the tag information onto a sales slip, manually transfer the information to stock record cards, and from there produce the various management reports, records, and decisions. In the IC segment, you will wave a pen-like device, called a wand, over a bar code tag on jewelry, automatically transfer

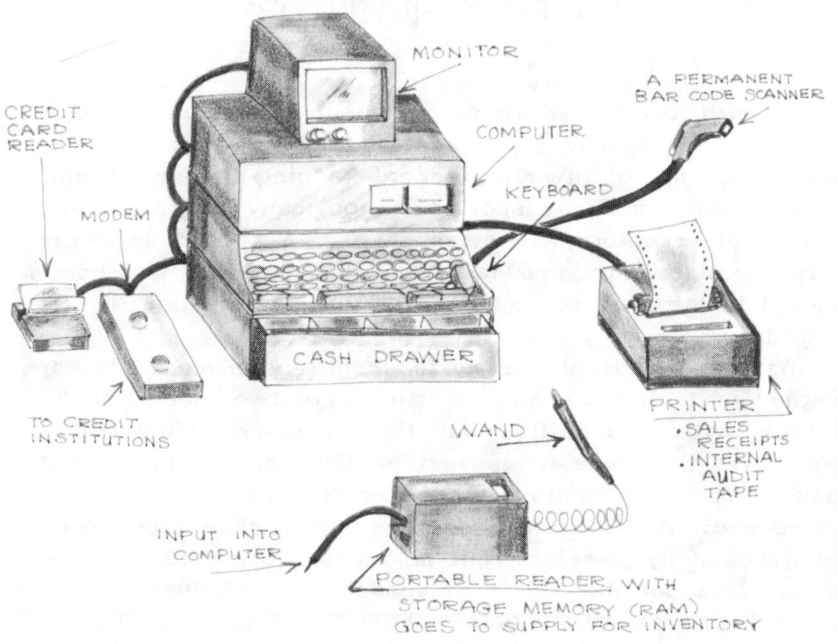

POINT OF SALE

Figure 2.8.4

all the tag's information into a portable bar code reader, and upload it to the computer, in which all segments will be updated.

If you decide that the POS is not cost-effective, you can use remote data entry, which will take place after the sale. You can assign one clerk to the entry-of-sales information into the computer, and at the same time use a less sophisticated cash register to fulfill the immediate needs of the sale.

TAKING INVENTORY

As with any record-keeping system, I recommend that, if you decide to use an IC system for your store, you assign the job of inventory record-keeping to one person. Just as the broth was spoiled by too many cooks, losing control of inventory will mean chaos. A second and third person can be assigned as a back up, but only one person should be directly responsible for the maintenance of records.

Without a portable bar code scanner, the most accurate method of taking inventories is to have two teams, each with a writer and caller, take the inventory. Each team goes over the same items as the other, but at a different time. When the results are tallied, the differences will be reconciled. This method takes longer than those commonly used by jewelers, but produces the greatest accuracy. If a portable bar code reader is used, two teams won't be necessary to obtain the same accuracy. The person taking the inventory then has only to ensure that each item in inventory passes under the wand and that the portable scanner accepts it.

BAR CODES

Most of us are familiar with bar codes. They are imprinted on most products we buy at stores. Adopted in 1973, the Universal Product Code (UPC) symbol was the first standard symbology used in bar codes. The UPC, a ten-digit number (the first five of which represent the supplier and the last five, the item number) is the most widely know symbology and is used primarily on groceries, books, records and magazines. Two more numbers can be added for further use. The UPC is the same as the European Article Number code, except for added characters that represent the country of origin.

Spacing and Width of Each Bar Give
Special Meaning These are read by
the Bar Code Scanners

SAMPLE BAR CODE

Figure 2.8.5

CODABAR, another widely used code, has special symbols and numbers. It is used by the Library of Congress, on medical blood bags and photofinishing bags.

Code 39, a registered trademark of Intermec Corporation, is an alpha-numeric code -- its symbols represent both letters and numbers. CODE 39 can be read in two directions with a bar code scanner; it can also be variable in length. Code 39 means "3 of 9" or each character is nine elements: 3 of which either spaces or bars will be wide.

Above, we discussed assigning stock numbers to jewelry in the IC segment of the I.J.P.. In the IC segment, you can also attach miniature bar codes on jewelry tags. A wand or bar code scanner will then read the code at the cash register and a portable scanner will read it for inventories. At the register, the transaction into the computer will take place automatically.

The advantage of the bar code POS system is that it reduces error and increases efficiency. A pleasant looking bar code tag, a portable inventory scanner and wand, a cash register, and the Ideal Jewelry Program Program's IC segment are all that is needed to make your life easier. You will tote the scanner around to each case, sweep the jewelry once with the scanner, listen for the familiar beep (indicating the information was accepted by the machine) and the jewelry will be recorded. Later this will be downloaded into the computer for posting to the IC segment.

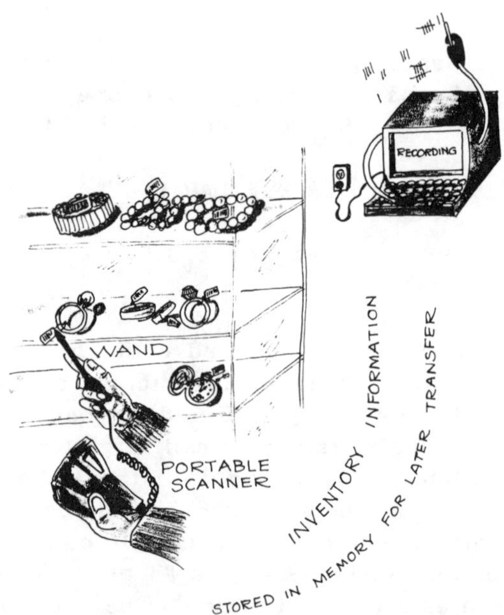

TAKING INVENTORY USING PORTABLE BAR CODE SCANNER

Figure 2.8.6

How will the salesperson know the price, manufacturer, cost, and quality? The price, quality, and size will be on the tag. For cost, manufacturer, date brought into stock, and so forth, the salesperson will look to the computer or to the computer generated stock book for this information. Your salesperson will find the suggested retail price, the minimum selling price, the cost (if you want the cost listed), a description of the item including sizes, qualities, manufacturer, and so forth. The bar code will be cross referenced in the computer program with all the above information.

As the portability of scanners increase, miniaturization of bar codes increase, and prices of POS systems decrease, you will soon be in the same league as large firms who have been using bar code technology for years. The major drawback to overcome is to make the technology readily available at a modest price in a presentable package for use in a jewelry store environment. The Ideal Jewelry Program will overcome these hurdles and feature POS and bar code capabilities.

MERCHANDISE CONTROL

Large organizations will have a great need for an automatic stock tagging system; for most jewelers this will be too costly and inappropriate. Now, as always, most jewelers still tag each item by hand. Only the style of tags and the information contained on each tag differs. Although most are similar. Of course, the reason to tag jewelry is to give you the ID of the item and the salesperson the information necessary to sell the item: this will probably include stock number, identification of material and stones, cost (in code) and retail price. One major problem with tags is that they break, wear, or fall off. If tied on, they get in the way and look sloppy, unless they are hidden from sight.

The I.J.P. will incorporate an indelible tag -- one that won't break or wear off, look unsightly or be too big, and that will contain all this information in a miniature bar code.

How does the salesperson read it? As most jewelers have counter pads, cleaning cloths, calculators, and ring tray plugs at each counter, so will there be a bar code scanner, a device that looks like a portable diamond tester. Lean, small, but effective, the bar code scanner will give the information on its display. It will tell the salesperson everything he needed to know; and, it will be directly connected to the computer, which will provide even more information and will be an invaluable assistant during inventory. Beyond impressing the customer, the salesperson will never have any trouble reading a tag or wrongly misplacing a number on a sales receipt or inventory sheet.

How will the tags be produced? Your printer will produce them on specially prepared sheets. The sheet, made of opaque thin plastic, will have hundreds of miniature, hour glass shaped, punch out tags that will be folded and riveted to jewelry or stuck to larger gift items. A special section of the IC segment can be called up at any time to produce a tag on any item in stock. You can flag (select) the items on which you needs tags or you can print new tags on everything in stock.

One advantage to printing a page of tags at a time is the freedom it gives you to retag large sections of your inventory. By periodically selecting a section of inventory for retagging, you will quickly and almost effortlessly prevent tags from having that worn and ragged look, the look which will lead the customer to think a piece of jewelry ". . . has been around. . . !"

SALES ENTRY

When a store is computerized, the only information a salesperson needs to enter into the cash register is the customer's name, merchandise stock numbers, payment and tax information (where the jeweler opts to use a bar code system, all of this except the customer's name is entered automatically through the scanner).

At the cash register, the only information the salesperson need enter into the cash register will be the customer's name, merchandise stock number, payment, and tax information. Then, owing to the IC's connection to the other segments of the I.J.P., POS transaction will automatically update accounts payable upon receipt of goods, accounts receivable upon the charge of goods, and payroll upon the sale of goods by a salesperson on commission.

STOCK NUMBERS

Stock numbers give you the means to classify each unique item you carry. Many theories exist on how to identify jewelry by stock numbers. Certain systems work better when you are automated, others when you are non-automated. In a non bar code system, the size of the tags that can be reasonably used on jewelry present a limitation. The stock number must be kept small but still contain the information important to keeping track of the piece.

For the IC segment each part of the stock number will be of equal length and of similar format. For example, the stock number will be a 9 digit number (the larger the inventory and the greater the number of stores, the larger the stock number will need to be to properly identify a piece of jewelry -- I have chosen an arbitrary 9-digit number; you might find an 13-,11-, 7-, or 5-digit number suits you better). The first three numbers will be assigned to the class of jewelry. This "class" is a description of the item's product type, ie. gold ring, stone, size, and description.

A separate index will be provided by the IC segment to describe what these classes are. The 100 class will be the 14kt yellow gold, and 101 will be 14 kt yellow gold rings, and 111 will be 14kt yellow gold engagement rings. Diamonds will be 200; style 211 will be .80-.94ct VVS1, F color diamonds, round. The next two digits will represent a vendor code. Zero one (01) will be ABC diamond cutters, 02 will be CDF Gold Mounting Company. The remaining four digits will be a unique number that is assigned only to that one vendor's item. Where you you will run into trouble, for example, will be when you have two each, .38ct diamonds: the same quality can come from many different diamond cutters. If you want to track all your .80ct, VVS1, F diamonds and you have two separate suppliers for this same diamond, you will have two separate stock numbers for them (see Figure 2.8.7).

Thus, these numbers tell us that the diamonds are the same, but they come from different suppliers. If you then go to the master cross reference list that the I.J.P. provides, you will find that both of these stock numbers cross over to the same size, color, shape, and clarity diamond, but a separate supplier. The disadvantage lies in having too many stock numbers for the same item; the advantage lies in the ability to track that one item, from receipt through sale. It also means that you have more than one choice of stock numbers to order when buying that style of diamond. You may find that one supplier's diamonds, although the same as the other suppliers, is not selling as well. This may be because one diamond is too highly priced, the cut is not as good, or some other reason.

The I.J.P. IC segment helps you organize your stock using these significant meaning codes, which provide a standard by which all stock will be marked. Employees have an easier time reading the numbers, and high stock turn inventory will be more readily spotted. When you receive new stock, you will assign it a unique stock number. If it is something you already carry, you will trace the item by supplier's stock number to its unique stock number. You will know that you already have one in stock, one is on-order, and three were sold within the

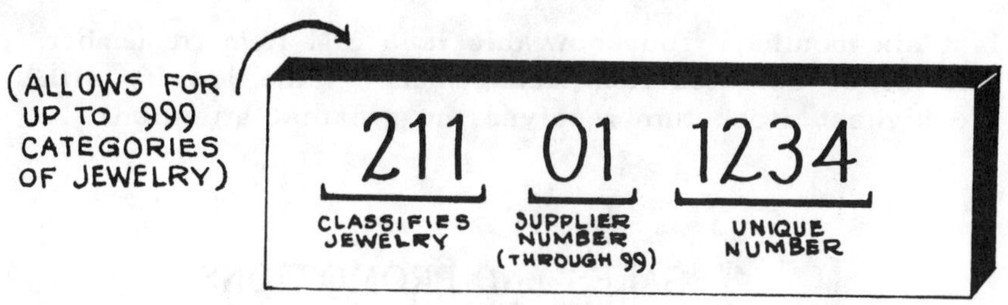

.80-.89 VVS1 or 2 F-G color
round diamonds

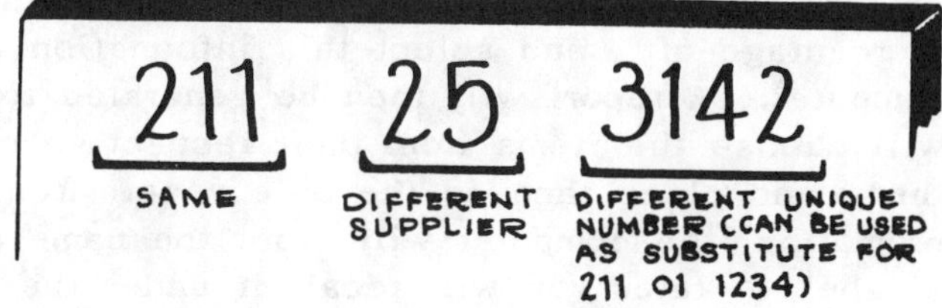

Assigning stock numbers to jewelry guarantees jeweler will always reassign all .80 - .89ct, VVS1 or 2, F - G color, round diamonds to same stock number every time same diamond is received from same supplier

Guarantees accurate SIM & NON-SIM information

STOCK DIAMONDS

Figure 2.8.7

last six months. You know this is a SIM item (remember this means Selected Item Management -- the jewelry with the highest stock turn receives the greatest attention).

SALES AND PROMOTIONS

Of the many useful tasks the IC segment performs, perhaps one of the most noteworthy is the variable pricing feature. When you have a promotion, you will pick the jewelry to be promoted. choose a fixed or variable "percentage-off", and select this information on the computer. A report will then be generated from which you will choose the items from their respective cases, tag them, and place them in the Sale case. You will name the promotion (the computer will store the name and use it as a label -- later you will recall it under the name you chose, ie. valentines 87') and even put effective dates for the promotion onto each item's inventory record. When the sale's date has passed the computer will no longer use the promotion prices set by you but revert back to the previously establish prices. If you later wanted a list of items you had on sale during the 1987 Valentine Promotion, it will be a keystroke away.

REPORTS

Table 2.8.2 gives a listing of the major reports that the IC segment will give you.

Part Number Listing
Master Cross Reference Jewelry Listing
Listing By Department Number,
  Description, Item Number, And Primary
   Vendor
Stock Status Listing
Order Recommendations
Inventory Analysis:
- Cost
- Price
- Margin
- Quantity on Hand
- Value
- On Hand Inventory
- Turn Over
- Shrinkages
- Overages
- SIM and NON-SIM Listing
- Cost of Sales

Inventory Transactions
Historical Cost Comparisons
Back Orders By Customer
Inventory Valuation
Computer Reorder Points
Listing Of All Backordered Items
Listing Of Cost Layers
Low Balance Items
Mailing List
Price List
Order Recommendations

INVENTORY REPORTS

Table 2.8.2

ECONOMIC ORDER QUANTITY (EOQ) AND STOCK ANALYSIS

A Bonus of the IC segment will be the inclusion of a special analysis section called Economic Order Quantity and Stock Analysis. Because the IC segment will monitor stock levels, it will recommend when to buy stock. If it sees that a certain pearl earring is a SIM item and is nearing a stock out situation, it will automatically recommend ordering the item for stock to a level that fits its demand. The Economic Order Quantity (EOQ) part of the IC segment will then establish the reorder quantity.

Also, the EOQ will help you to decide if vendor discount schemes were a good deal. Have you ever wondered if the six month memorandum is any better than taking the 2% net 10-day payment, or the 30-, 60-, 90- day payment methods? The EOQ will allow you to find the best terms for the most profit. On the exterior the terms may seem better; the EOQ will tell you which is truly the best in your situation.

Several features of the EOQ are worth noting. The EOQ helps to find savings on high cost and large volume items. Further, it will show inventory problems in time for you to act. As in the Spreadsheet segment, you will play "what-if" analysis by simulating variable demands on different stock items. In addition, the EOQ will calculate stockout probabilities, do cost analysis when historical inventory levels are not at their best, and most importantly, track supplier memorandums so you does not lose sight and keep memos longer than the allotted time frame.

Your IC Segment will contain the information listed in Table 2.8.3 on each of the items kept in stock.

Active (Or Inactive)
Allocated Stock (Stock On Order)
Date Of Last Sale
Description
General Ledger Code
Hits
Inventory Differences (On Hand Vs.
 Inventory Count Of Item Actually In Stock)
Last Order
Lead Time
Location
Minimum Level
NON-SIM
ONE HIT
Price Unit
Price Unit Description
Product Type
Promotion Name
Promotion Dates
Quantity Discount
Reorder Level
Selling Prices
SIM
Standard Cost
Stock Code
Stock Group
Stock On Hand
Tax Code (Is It Subject To Sales Tax?)
Terms DIscount
Trade Discount
Unit Weight
Vendor Reference

INVENTORY INFORMATION

Table 2.8.3

SECURITY

As you begin to depend more and more on the computer you might see the need to protect more important records from unscrupulous eyes. The IC segment has the means to do this. You may readily appoint yourself all levels of access to the computers files; whereas with others, you might limit to some degree or another -- you may not want Billy Bob or Betty Sue having access to the payroll or to the Inventory at Cost figures. The IC Segment of the I.J.P. will be designed to keep control in the your hands -- where it belongs.

Here we should stop for a minute and discuss how this is done. You may recall earlier we discussed local area networks and file locking. In addition, we discussed passwords. In the I.J.P., access to the files will be assigned by a super user or system custodian (yourself or the accountant or other qualified person). Before a person is allowed to use the computer, they will be trained on how to operate it and be given a special access code. The code will have hidden meaning because it will signify access of up to three levels to the I.J.P.

The first level will be "read only" (will only read files); the next level will be "write access" (all the rights of the first plus the person can erase and write information to the file); the third level of access is "execute" (here the user can do all of the first two levels and in addition, he can execute programs that can be run). In addition, each file has one owner -- usually the person who created the information in the file. It is this owner of a file who is given one of the three levels of access mentioned above. Other users may have access to the owners files but these will also be controlled by the above levels of access.

DEPARTMENTAL CONTROL

The IC Segment will be organized to allow you to control your store by department. By breaking down the control into smaller departmental areas, it will allow you to have greater rein on your inventory. This concept is not new, and will be an effective management tool.

PLAIN ENGLISH QUERY LANGUAGE

The value of the IC segment will be augmented by the quality of the reports it generates. Besides the reports listed in Table 2.8.2, the IC Segment will give the ability to query its data bases in plain English text. In other words, you will have the ability to ask question of the computer, such as, "List all watches sold within last two months over $2000 with greater than 15% discount by salesperson no. 3." The computer generates the report and you discover that no watches were sold with a discount greater than 15%. Now, perhaps you want to know how many watches over $2000.00 did salesperson no. 3 sell? You ask, "List all watches sold by salesperson three within last 2 months for over $2000." The computer answers six watches, all Rolex except for 1 Patek Phillip" -- I left out the stock numbers to conserve space. With the ability to ask the computer questions in plain English, you have a tool that will aid you in making wiser financial and management decisions.

For the I.J.P. to understand plain English, it must be programmed to understand all the different syntaxes it will meet. At the surface this may seem easy, but it is not. Think of all the different ways the same question can be asked. As computers become smarter and inroads are made into artificial intelligence, programs that will have near human-like qualities of plain English text recognition will become more widely available. At present, some programs have pseudo-English command structures, but require you to learn the syntax. Thus, the computer is requiring us to learn its syntax instead of its learning ours.

The computer can't understand everyone ... too many languages and dialicts...we must learn how to speak computer language...at least for awhile. . .

WE STILL HAVE TO LEARN COMPUTER TALK

Figure 2.8.8

AN IC OVERVIEW

In short, what will the IC segment do for you? First, it will give you increased accuracy, greater control, and a balanced inventory. It will enable you to bank the 18% to 25% estimated cost of carrying any excess inventory. Second, it will give you control of your stock turn -- therefore your profit. Third, because of strict insurance company requirements to keep accurate inventory records, you will rest nights knowing that your inventory is properly documented. A computerized IC segment is not the solution to all of your store management problems, but through the use of sound inventory control procedures, you will yet reach another ring.

9

ACCOUNTS RECEIVABLE

DISCUSSION OF TERMS

AVERAGE COLLECTION PERIOD--The average mumber of days account receivable dollars stay outstanding. This helps analysts to determine the chances of collecting a firm's receivables.

BALANCE FORWARD--A method used in the Accounts Receivable segment of accounting software that brings the balance only forward to the next accounting period. This is in lieu of bringing the details of that account forward (see OPEN ITEM) into the next accounting period.

CASH CONVERSION CYCLE--Represents the time involved in converting a sale into cash on hand. The quicker this cycle is, the better the cash flow posture of the business.

TERMS CODE--Predefined series of codes representing various terms of credit sales, and so forth.

OPEN ITEM--A method used in the Accounts Receivable portion of some accounting software that keeps the details of an account open from accounting period to accounting period. This differs from the balance forward method (see BALANCE FORWARD).

The Accounts Receivable segment of the Ideal Jewelry Program allows you to reduce outside data processing costs. Of course, the AR segment will be flexible enough to adjust to your billing policies, and at the same time will give you the power of a sophisticated billing system, enabling you to keep track of as many clients as you will ever need.

The beauty of the Accounts Receivable (AR) segment is the way it interacts with the other parts of the Ideal Jewelry Program. With it, you will print professional, customized invoices that allows a personalized or promotional message to the customer. Just like the Inventory Control segment, it will be integrated with the Spreadsheet and Word Processor. Too, the AR segment has the same powerful, plain English commands that is available in the other segments, whereby you will make customized reports to suit special requirements you may have.

The AR segment will be menu driven and it will be easy to set up and use. The program first asks you questions about your business. Once answered, the program is configured for your business. If at any time you desire to change, for example, the billing cycle, you merely have to call up the system management file of the program and reanswer the questions in the desired manner.

At each stage in the program, it prompts you with choices and you can decide what work to do at that time. So, if you want to enter a client into the program for the first time, you will be asked the information in Table 2.9.1 (thank goodness for credit application forms).

Each entry will commensurate with a prescribed set of codes. For example, the zip code is the zip code where the customer lives (the computer is programmed to accept 7-digit zip codes). But, the transaction date is a 4-digit julian date (the first digit stands for the last digit of the current year, and the last 3-digits stand for the number of days since the first day of the year. For example, 6001 is January 1, 1986; of course, you have to make the assumption in which decade you are. Here is another example: 7031 is January 31, 1987. This format guarantees standardization throughout the program. How will you know the julian date? The program will have a julian date calendar built into it; all you need do will be to request the julian date and the computer will tell you).

Likewise, the terms code will be a predefined series of 5 codes (these were defined in the question and answer segment when first using the program). Each of these codes gives you the flexibility to bill each customer according to a different set of sales terms as some customers need more flexible financing than others. Further information on the meanings of the codes is available by pushing the designated "help" button on the computer. So, if you don't understand a command or a code, then simply ask the computer for help. The on-line help function is a useful aid offered by most major programs. The easier the program is to learn, the more it buoys up learning -- the better it will suit you.

The higher the quality of information in reports, the better use you will make of them. Reports give you the management tools you need to forge decisions. For example, the average collection period plays the largest part in the cash conversion cycle, which is converting receivables to dollars; your policy on this will have a large effect on the health of your collections. If you have a lax collection and credit policy with a long average collection period you will see your bad-debt write-offs swell.

The AR reports of the Ideal Jewelry Program enables you to grasp control of your average collection period, reduce your bad-debt write-offs, and increase sales through increased positive contact with the customer. The AR segment is connected with the Point of Sale Electronic Funds Transfer System (EFTS), part of the Ideal Jewelry Program's Inventory Control segment. Of

Account Balance
Account Numbers
Account Type
Age, Wife's Name
Amount Last Debit
Amount Last Credit
Any Comments
Assigned Salesperson
Birthdays, And Other Personal Information
City
City Sales Tax
Client Or Company Name
County Sales Tax
Credit Limit
Date Last Credit
Date Last Debit
Discount Date
Discount Percentage
Due Date
Invoice Number
Product Description
Product Stock Number
Sales Tax Codes
Service Charge Code
State
State Sales Tax
Street Address
Taxable/Exempt
Telephone
Terms Codes
Transaction Amount
Transaction Date
Type Of Business Or Occupation
YTD Credits
YTD Debits
Zip Code

ACCOUNTS RECEIVABLE DATA

Table 2.9.1

course, quicker turn-around time for credit approvals lops time off the cash conversion cycle. Figure 2.9.2 shows the cash conversion cycle. The sooner this money can be put into the business, the better the cash flow; anything you can do to quicken, at any step in the cycle, the tempo of your AR, the greater the bottom line profit will be.

There are other useful reports in this segment as well. For instance, look at the Client Profile Analysis report. This will tell you who your credit customers are, where they live, what their incomes are, and more. It allows you to more easily focus your marketing onus to this group of customers. You can put promotional messages and mailers in with each monthly statement. After having carefully analyzed your market, you can bait your invoices with well-suited hooks that will bring in more sales. Table 2.9.2 lists other reports of the AR segment.

Aged Trial Balances
Average Collection Period Report
Billing Messages
Client Numeric and Alphabetic Account Number Listings
Client Profile Analysis
Company or Client Data
Department Code and Description Report
Detailed and Summary Client Master
Detailed and Summary Payment Register
Detailed and Summary Salesman Reports
Detailed and Summary Ticket Registers
General Ledger Interface
Mailing List
Production Analysis Reports by Department Codes
Salesman or Client Number

AR SEGMENT REPORTS

Table 2.9.2

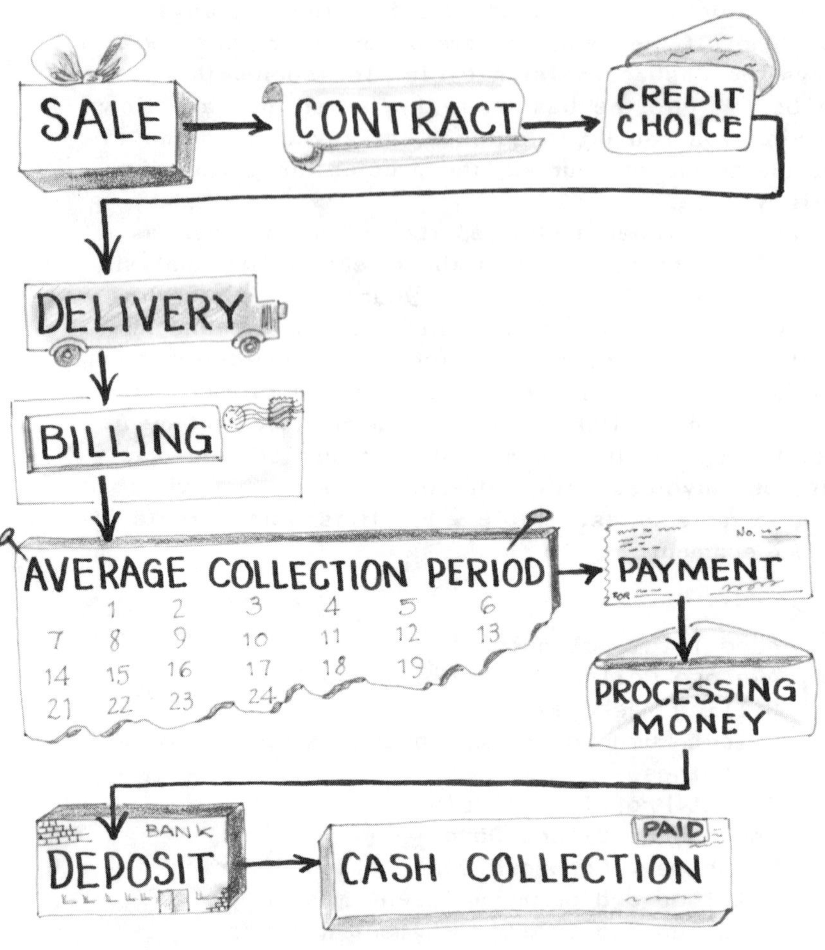

CASH CONVERSION CYCLE

Figure 2.9.1

Figure 2.9.2 gives a sample of possible menus that the AR segment will use.

An added feature of the AR segment is that it allows the choice of accounting period. If you decide your fiscal year should run differently from the calendar year, this program will facilitate that.

The AR segment automatically computes finance charges based on the agreement of terms and the term code (see above). Some credit terms may mean greater risks

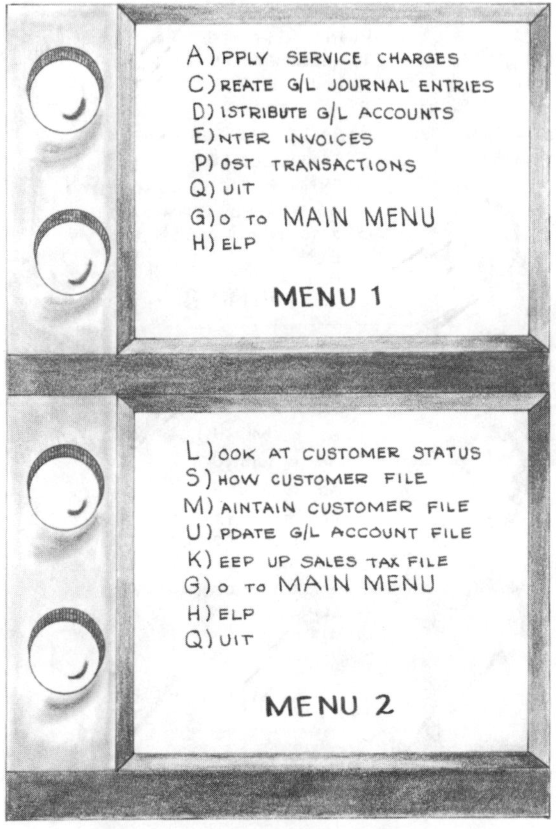

SAMPLE MENUS

Figure 2.9.2a

on your part in which case the gain should be greater. The AR segment allows for this and automatically computes different terms for the specified clients. The AR segment also allows for the choice of accounting methods, either the Open Item or Balance Forward method. And it allows for variable aging of accounts and gives aged accounts reports. Certified Public Accountants

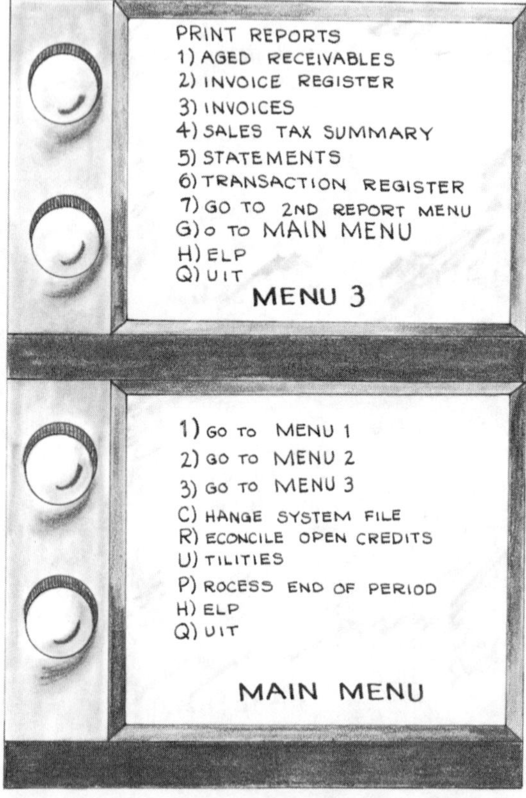

SAMPLE MENUS

Figure 2.9.2b

and the IRS will also appreciate the audit trail the AR segment leaves: it will be easy to follow, complete, and well-documented.

Lastly, because it will only be limited in the number of clients by the storage capacity of the computer, because it will interface directly with the Word Processor and Spreadsheet segments of the Ideal Jewelry Program, and because it will have an on-line help tutorial, you will find it to be extremely friendly and useful.

10

ACCOUNTS PAYABLE

The next important program segment of the I.J.P. is Accounts Payable (AP). The AP segment will be a bookkeeper's dream come true; for they will save all the space normally kept for the account cards, and all those checks they once had to write by hand will now be printed by printer.

The AP segment is integrated with the other segments of the I.J.P., from Word Processor through General Ledger. Its major benefit is time savings -- the AP segment keeps track of the discount periods and other important information on vendors, and calculates vendor discounts and total purchase prices of the goods and services you buy. It will also calculate the float period.

What is the float period? It is the time that remains from when the check is written to the time that the bank has drawn on your account funds to pay against it. This float period varies, usually by days, and sometimes by a week or more. Thus, the AP segment will keep cash in the business for a longer period giving you an enhanced cash flow situation. Following the wine industry's well known adage, "Sell no wine before its time", so you should pay no bill before its time. Not that you should delay payment of your bills past their due date or disregard vendor discounts when applicable, but you should keep your dollars working in your business for as long a time as possible. The AP segment will be programmed to track, calculate, and make recommendations to take advantage of the float period.

Not being able to easily support handwritten checks is a major complaint of those who use automated AP program's, but a complaint that won't be heard about this AP segment. The AP segment of the I.J.P. will make it easy to disburse hand written checks. The bookkeeper need only write the check and post the transaction in the AP segment; the AP segment automatically registers the transaction and include it in the month's end reports and registers.

Disk Storage, like the other program segments, is the only limit on the amount of accounts the AP segment will accept. By adding more storage, you will be able to open and close as many accounts as you will need. The segment is designed to give a complete audit trail of all transactions including old accounts. Also, like the other segments, this segment is menu driven with easy-to-use and friendly menus, and eventually should have a plain English command syntax available if you needs special reports. It will give you variable aging, be flexible in meeting the needs of your operation, have on-line help tutorials, and will have full data editing features.

Full data-editing features are important, because they let the bookkeeper correct a mistake at the time of discovery. Along with this, the program will have strong error handling capabilities. For example, if the bookkeeper makes an entry error, the AP segment will not crash (shut down) the computer; it will merely beep and tell the bookkeeper to correctly enter the data. In most cases the program will avoid these entry errors altogether, because the programmers will have formatted the data entry screen to take into consideration errors a bookkeeper will make during data entry.

The AP segment is designed to produce a check register, record invoices, and automatically post periodically due invoices. Based on your desires, the AP segment automatically purges historical data. It will credit and debit memos and open credits. And, in addition to the ordinary accounts, it will handle fixed term and perpetual payment accounts.

As an Open System (see OPEN ITEM in glossary) it will: keep the balance due by invoice for greatest control, verify the balance against a master balance for security, and, lastly, let you run reports as often as necessary.

A typical month might go like this. First, you will enter any new vendors into the computer. As necessary, the bookkeeper will record invoices, credit memos, debit memos, and open any credits. Based on the Priority Code assigned when the vendor was first put into the AP segment, the bookkeeper will select those vendors you wanted to pay. Remember that floating for as long as possible without, and I repeat, without offending the vendors is important to the cash flow of the firm.

The bookkeeper will then ask the computer for the float report and for a list of vendors that should be paid now. With these reports, you will be able to delay your cash outflow as long as possible and still support a tight, controlled, and prompt payment schedule.

Next in the monthly cycle, the bookkeeper will send payments to the vendors. At the end of the cycle the bookkeeper will generate the reports listed in Table 2.10.1, and lastly, will clear the monthly files and transfer the accumulated accounts to the General Ledger segment of the I.J.P. Of course, at any time you can choose to send a customized letter to your bank that will use the Word Processor, Graphics, and Spreadsheet segments to present your financial position in a professional, concise package, one with which the bank will be impressed. This will be useful if you needed additional capital to fill in your cash flow posture for, let's say, a 35 day period.

Cash Requirements By Pay Date and Vendor Name
Cash Requirement Forecast
Check Book Register by G/L Period and Check Number
Check Register by Check Number
Customer Profile
Float Period Report
Mailing List
Name and Address by Vendor Name or Number
Open Voucher Listing by Vendor Name and Invoice Date
Report of Mail Due Date for Each Vendor
Transaction File Listing
Voucher Booking Register by G/L Period and Vendor Name
Voucher Detail Register by Voucher Number

REPORTS OF ACCOUNTS PAYABLE SEGMENT

Table 2.10.1

Table 2.10.2 gives you an example of the information the AP segment includes on the vendors.

Account number
Address
Check sent
City
Cur. A/P Balance
Date check marked paid
Flagged to pay
Name
Open Credits
Pay date
Priority (how important is it to pay?)
State
Term code (what is your credit arrangement?)
Type(4 digit code corresponding to merchandise carried)
YTD Paid
YTD purchases
Zip Code

INFORMATION KEPT ON VENDORS

Table 2.10.2

11

GENERAL LEDGER

DISCUSSION OF TERMS

PROOF VALUES--An error checking feature used in balancing accounts.

RATIO ANALYSIS--Technique used to compare business profits with overhead costs to get an accurate picture of a business's health. Ratio analysis, for the most part, is performed through simple mathematical analysis of key accounting data. A profit and loss statement provides much useful information for Ratio Analysis.

The General Ledger (GL) Segment of the I.J.P. is the glue that holds the old-fashioned filing cabinet together. Jewelers have used accounting services, bookkeepers, and accountants for years, and for years they have asked:

> "Is my business profitable? How much profit have I made? Will I be in the black this month? This year? Will it be as good next year?"

The GL segment receives its input from the other Ideal Jewelry Program's segments; it automatically posts, processes, and packages the raw data into a useful format. From the GL's segment and its reports, you will extract information that will aid you in making wise decisions for months ahead.

In the past, the Profit and Loss (P&L) Statement will be several weeks to months in coming; now, the P&L, generated on your computer, will be on your desk in a matter of hours or days. Naturally, its timeliness will enable you to make real-time decisions in the operation of your business.

What is the GL segment? Simply, it tracks the accounts you set up in your business. In the I.J.P., these accounting segments will not replace the accountant or accounting principles; they will merely speed up the process of accounting. This frees time for you to plan your business's future, rather than mull over laborious paperwork.

Even with a computer, however, it's possible to make unwise business decisions; it is still up to you to know how to interpret the information produced by these segments. I mentioned earlier about impressing the banks with the professional nature in which the "books" are kept at your business, both in their appearance and their accuracy. If you are thinking of growth and have to call upon outside financing, the information that the GL segment produces will be important. The income statement and the balance sheet will be your barometers. Knowing how to interpret the information provided by all the Accounting segments of the I.J.P. will be your key to success. Learning to turn that key will enable you to open the door to a business that is trim, competitive, and profitable.

With the arrival of automated accounting, comparative analysis of statements is made painless. Trend spotting is a by-product of automatic accounting design. Ratio analysis of which we, spoke in the Spreadsheet segment, is the analysis of accounting data and will act as a barometer to the business's health. As this is not an accounting manual, further information can be sought from your accountant and in several good books on these subjects.

The GL segment of the I.J.P. will give you an on-line tutorial that assists in the analysis of the reports produced by the GL segment. For example, two especially useful features of the GL segment will be comparison of budgeted figures to actual figures and comparison of Year-to-Date (YTD) figures between accounting periods that will include an absolute and a percent change figure. This will be done for both quarterly reports and year ago comparisons. Further, you can cross over the data from the GL segment to the Spreadsheet segment of the I.J.P. providing you with a powerful analysis tool. The ratio analysis template that will be provided with the spreadsheet will permit you to take your business's temperature; your accountant can help give you a prognosis or give you a Business Health Seal of Approval.

The GL segment will be full of useful features that will speed the accounting functions of your business. For example the GL segment gives all account activity with beginning and ending balances. You can always run reports to the printer or to the screen. Owing to the built in error-checking features called proof values, the GL segment will always remain in balance. This does not mean that something will not be posted to the wrong account, but that the credits will always match the debits.

Also, the GL segment will be menu driven, have password security, self-formatting reports, numerous subtotal levels available, and receive posting information directly from the Accounts Payable, the Accounts Receivable, the Inventory Control, and the Payroll segments of the I.J.P.. These features will save the bookkeepers days of work.

Through the computer, you can establish an unlimited number of accounts, and you can have as many as 10 checking accounts and 13 accounting periods. A year-end feature will clear all profit and loss account activity, join balance sheet transactions into a beginning balance for the new year, and roll the year end account totals over into last year comparative figures. You can even establish your own accounting periods. Lastly, the GL segment will handle zero balance and inactive accounts.

A typical monthly cycle in the GL segment is presented in Table 2.11.1.

Daily routine:
- Enter transactions, print control report
- Delete incorrect transactions, print control report
- Save and store control reports

Weekly:
- Make backup copies of Data
- Print and save Transaction register

Monthly:
- Transfer Summary Journals, if applicable
- Print Transaction Register of current month activity
- Print Detail Trial Balance
- Print Balance Sheet
- Print Income Statement
- Process End of Period

Yearly:
- Clear account activity
- Join balance sheet transaction into beginning balance for new year

MONTHLY CYCLE

Table 2.11.1

The quality of the GL segment will also rest with the accuracy of the accounting, and the quality of the reports. Table 2.11.2 lists the reports that will be included in the GL segment of the Ideal Jewelry Program. These reports allow you to keep a complete audit trail of your accounting, see your Profit and Loss Statements on time, and locate and correct any accounting or related problems.

In short, the GL segment allows your computer to handle the drudgery of bookkeeping and frees you to do what you do best -- market jewelry.

Allows on-line GL account detail inquiry
Balance Sheet
Balance sheet Chart of Accounts
Check Register
Consolidated Income Statements
Detail History Report
Detail Trial Balance
Entry Exception Report
Entry Journals
Journal Listing
Journal Voucher Register
Prints The Trial Balance And Working Trial Balance
Profit and Loss Statement Source Cross Reference
Report (by SOURCE CODE Or Account Number, Shows All Transactions For The Current Accounting Period For Selected Sources: The SOURCE CODE Shows The Origin Of The Transaction, ie. AR, AP, IC And The Rest)
Sub-scheduled Reports

REPORTS

Table 2.11.2

12

PAYROLL

Wouldn't it be nice to say good bye to those days when paychecks had to be done by hand? With the I.J.P.'s Payroll segment you will do all that and more.

Perhaps the most important feature of this segment, like other segments, is it degree of protection from unauthorized access. You may recall the three layer password protection discussed in the Introduction to the I.J.P. This protects data from over-zealous employees, should they decide to penetrate important information. An additional option available to you in this segment of the I.J.P. will be an optional data encryption routine that will prevent a person, even after garnering a copy of the data, from learning the information -- it will be garbled until the correct code was given to unscramble it. And, since the information contained in this segment is especially sensitive, this will be particularly important.

Wouldn't this be overdoing it? The computer makes it easy to make copies of all files. Thus, its crucial to do everything possible to keep even the most determined of individuals away from these records. With the total reliance on a computer to keep all the bookkeeping and important files, it simply makes sense to take proper precautions to protect your investment of time, money, and convenience.

The Payroll segment is full of features that make it easy to use and follow. Data is entered with ease and errors will be corrected smoothly, quickly, and reliably.

For example, the Payroll segment allows you to preview (see reports on the monitor instead of on a printer) all reports to the screen. This can be done at anytime in the Payroll cycle. Like other segments, Payroll is menu driven with an underlying plain English command syntax. This will make the segment flexible: a beginner can use the system and a seasoned bookkeeper can extract custom reports. In other words, it will be designed like an onion. Beneath each layer, another layer awaits. The outer layer will be what most people see; yet, underneath the outer layer a full spectrum of layers exist that give you capability upon capability. This segment, like the others, will have a "help" tutorial that you can call up with the push of one button.

Most jewelers realize that, even though the Payroll segment will print checks, some checks will still have to be handwritten. The Payroll segment will account for this situation minimizing the bookkeeper's paperwork and reporting requirements. It will incorporate proof values so it will always remain in balance. Further, it will feature a detailed audit trail with which CPA's and IRS agents will be most pleased. It will handle up to 999 employees, 8 miscellaneous deductions, special pay and overtime (including 1.5x, 2.0x, 2.25x...), workmen's compensation premium calculations, zero balance and inactive employees, voided payroll checks, special pay between pay periods, and non-taxable employees.

The Payroll segment will be programmed to account for multiple companies. Within a company it will be capable of department and job cost accounting. It will handle hourly, salaried, and monthly employees, from a variety of states, and include user maintainable federal and state tax tables for as many states as storage will allow. It will even handle nonstandard tax deductions.

This segment will also give you flexibility in paying commissions: you can choose to include spiffs, draw, and split sales. This will give you the ability to reward top salespeople and to move slow moving merchandise.

As with the other segments of the I.J.P., the Payroll segment will be integrated with the Spreadsheet and Word Processor segments enabling you to analyse data and produce custom reports as needed.

In addition to wages year to date and tax information, the Payroll will keep employee information as listed in Table 2.12.1.

Additional Information the Jeweler Wants to Keep
Address
Children's Names and Birthdays
Date Employed
Department
Exemptions
Filing Status
Home Address
Phone Number of Nearest Relative
Miscellaneous
Deductions
Name
Pay Rate
Pay Type
Shift
Sick Days Taken
Social Security Number
Telephone Number
Vacation Days Taken
Wife's Name and Birthday

PAYROLL INFORMATION

Table 2.12.1

Having this information on each employee, you will keep track of the important employee information, such as birthday's, anniversaries, date of last pay raise, and so forth.

Check Register
Current Quarter and Year to Date Earnings Report
Deduction Register
Detailed Employee Files
Employee mailing labels
Labor Distribution Register
Master Edit List
Materials Register
Materials and Labor History Report
Monthly Payroll Summary
Monthly Report Totals by Departments for posting
  to GL
Pay Limits Report
Payroll Payment Journal
Payroll checks with stubs
Piecework Report
Quarterly Payroll Summary
Quarterly Reports: For 941 For W-2 Employee Earning
  Register
Quarterly Unemployment Report
Quarterly Withholding Report
Sick Leave and Vacation Report
Task Summary Report
Time Card Register
Time Ticket Journal
W-2 forms

REPORTS

Table 2.12.2

You can generate a birthday report, a special employee report, and keep any other information on the employee that might help you. Table 2.12.2 lists more reports of the Payroll segment.

Table 2.12.3 gives a general overview of the typical pay period cycle.

Each Pay Period
Enter Payroll
Enter wage distribution
Job cost distribution
General journal
Print checks
Print copies of the Payroll register,
 check register, and general journal
Check key items against time sheets, expense
 reports for accuracy
Execute the post command
Make backup of the data
Execute end of pay period command

PAY CYCLE

Table 2.12.3

13

DIAMOND SALES DEMONSTRATION IN 3-D GRAPHICS

DISCUSSION OF TERMS

PIXEL(Picture element)--The smallest point on a computer monitor that can be manipulated by the computer's program.

ALIASING--The step effect created by the low resolution of some computer monitors. The higher the resolution, the less stepping is evident.

PORTABILITY--Ability of a program or operating system to be used in more than one type of computer without major revision. Programs must be written with portability in mind otherwise a program written in a portable language may not be as portable as one might think. "C" language and Modula 2 are examples of portable languages and UNIX is an example of a portable operating system, which was written mostly in the "C" language.

AMERICAN STANDARD CODE FOR INFORMATION INTERCHANGE (ASCII)--A set of symbols number from 1 to 128 that account for most of the symbols used on modern typewriters and keyboards. First established in the era of teletype machines, the use of this code ensures that other computers will understand the information sent from one computer to another. Some IBM mainframe computers use a standard set of code called EBCDIC. It is similar to but not the same as ASCII. If a computer that uses ASCII and another EBCDIC, for them to share data one or the other or both computers will have to convert the code so that it will be understood by the other computer.

In this chapter and the following chapter, we will be discussing several programs that have not yet been developed or that have been developed but are not widely known to exist. Owing to their nature, these are a natural tool for jewelers to use in their everyday work environment and will someday be available for use.

Computers need large amounts of Random Access Read-Write Memory (RAM) to create high resolution graphics. Graphics programs address each pixel, the smallest point on a computer monitor that can be manipulated by the computer's program. The greater the number of pixels the computer can manipulate the greater the density or resolution of the image. A typical computer might have a resolution of 640 X 200 pixels. A line produced by a computer with this resolution will be slightly jagged; this is called aliasing. The higher the resolution the less the aliasing will be, until, eventually, when the resolution is high enough, the stepping -- or jaggedness -- disappears. At the point where the aliasing disappears, images can be created on the computer monitor that rival the quality of lithographic illustrations.

Due to the nature of each computer's microprocessor, graphics programs that work on one computer will not work on another computer unless the program is tailored to the special structure of the computer or the computers are compatible with each other (this normally means that the computers share the same microprocessor and are programmed in nearly the same manner so that programs will run on one or the other with no modification). Knowing that portability, the ability of the program to run on more than one kind of computer, is the most important hallmark of the I.J.P., the graphics part of the program will then have to be written in such a manner as to make porting from computer A to computer B easy. The 3-dimensional graphics presentation of diamonds and colored stones on the computer will be limited to certain brands of computers, at least until a universal and powerful graphics language does surface.

Hope does exist, though. The North American Presentation Level Protocol Syntax (NAPLPS) is a standardized means of coding graphics so that they can be used on two different brands of computers. NAPLPS is similar in purpose to the American Standard Code for Information Exchange (ASCII) and is used primarily in Videotext applications. Both NAPLPS and ASCII allow the transfer of information via a modem. NAPLPS permits the transfer of graphics over the phone or a television signal. It creates images by a standardized set of instructions that create simple lines, circles, and colors. What does all this have to do with you? You will use the computer's graphics capabilities to teach and demonstrate a diamond's color, cut, and clarity. You will also use it to plot inclusions and proportions of diamonds for the Appraisal sub-section of the Inventory Control segment. You now use many different audio-visual aids in the sale of a diamond or colored stone to a customer. You can use a proportion scope, a binocular microscope, a television monitor attached to a binocular microscope camera, pictures of different diamonds, and even actual diamonds and colored stones. Each tool serves to individualize and professionalize your service.

A computer, with the right program, will display light as it travels through the diamond. Through the push of key you will rotate the diamond, change its proportions, and show its identifying characteristic inclusions, its colors, and it hidden facets. So why not use a computer to demonstrate the 4C's of the diamond?

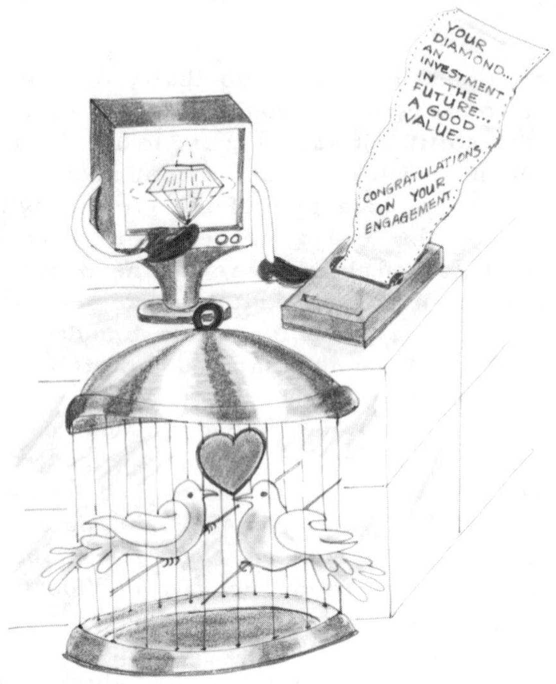

THE DIAMOND DEMONSTRATION

Figure 2.13.1

In the I.J.P., you will have a computer monitor and keyboard available to you in your sales presentation area. With these, you will graphically show the path that light takes in travelling through the diamond. Further, you will show the customer how minute changes in a diamond's proportions will affect the beauty of a diamond. You will rotate the diamond on the screen in a manner that the customer will see the complexity and beauty of the diamond. You will show the customer how diamond grading effects the price of a diamond. By changing the shading of the diamond and moving around inclusions in the 3-Dimensional view of the diamond on the screen, the you will give the customer an interactive sales presentation. You will take the diamond that the customer is thinking of buying, create a 3-D diamond image that closely resembles that diamond, and provide the customer with a printed copy of his chosen diamond.

Not all customers may need such a sophisticated presentation to be closed, but some might -- especially if the jeweler at the other end of the mall uses the computer to inform his customers about diamonds and colored stones!

14

TOOL TO PROFITABILITY & PRODUCTIVITY

In making a major jewelry purchase, the jewelry buying public considers reputation most important: you should do everything in your power to enhance your image before the public. Store traffic is a direct result of location and advertising. The ratio of sold customers to total store traffic distinguishes the profit makers from the hangers on. If you do not close a high enough percentage of your traffic to pay your bills, then you should ask yourself, "What am I doing wrong?"

The Ideal Jewelry Program will give you a greatly enhanced means to remain within the minds of your customers, both present and future. It is a tool of profitability--a tool designed to keep track of customers, inventory, repairs, sales, and more. A computer will help get new customers (Mailing List), it will help keep current customers (Customer Data Base), and it will help close more customers (follow ups and monitoring employee incentives and bonuses).

Learning the features of the imaginary Ideal Jewelry Program will give you a taste for the capabilities and potential of computers. It will address the areas from which you can derive the greatest benefit.

The way you buy and sell jewelry is changing. You are no longer able to deliberate on the swelling economy and throes of an ever-increasing inflation rate. You have to cleverly market your wares. Good marketing technique separates the profitable jeweler from the unprofitable. The Ideal Jewelry Program will give you the advantage you need to maintain profitability, and the tools you need to increase productivity.

The future is ever close at hand with computers. Every year brings dramatic changes and ever more useful software and computers. Below we will discuss several areas -- some that exist now and others that do not -- that will give you an ever greater potential for increased productivity.

Productivity

Let's pause for a few minutes and look at the how the Ideal Jewelry Program will help improve the productivity of your staff. The I.J.P. has all of the standard software necessary to run a business, ie. payroll, inventory control, and so forth. Yet, in addition, it will have the ability to run programs that will make your managers better managers, your salespeople better salespeople, and your appraisers better appraisers. How?

THE GEMOLOGIST'S WORKBENCH

With the push on by both internal and external organizations, the jewelry appraiser is required more and more to be licensed or certified or trained to very high standards. Several organizations exist that strive to fill these needs. The American Gem Society has the Certified Gemologist Appraiser program. The Gemological Appraisal Association offers three titles for appraisers. The International Society of Appraiser has the Certified Appraiser of Personal Property Program (CAPP). The Gemological Institute of America trains thousands of gemologists and jewelers per year in the science of gem identification, grading, and in diamond grading. The gemologist's workbench will be a program of the Ideal Jewelry Program that will facilitate the desires of all these organizations to make the trained jeweler/appraiser more professional, proficient, and prepared to meet the challenge of the future.

What is the gemologist's workbench? How will this program help you? The gemologist's workbench will be a series of programs designed around the needs of an appraiser and gemologist. Part one of the the gemologist's workbench is the the gem identification and appraisal section. Here the gemologist will enter information regarding the properties of a gemstone or diamond. The program will, using artificial intelligence techniques, provide an identification of the gemstone. If just the measurements are known, it will compute the approximate weight. Using the GIA colored stone grading system or the GIA diamond grading system, the program will provide the price of the stones.

The workbench will have an on line help file that will provide insight and answers to the latest in legal information and methodology. And this information can be called up from anywhere from with the program. The jeweler could ask, "For purposes of federal taxes, at what value should I appraise this diamond and platinum ring?" "What are the appropriate tax laws under which I'm held responsible?" "What is the additional information that I have to submit along with the appraisal?"

Next, you will be guided to provide a description of the jewelry and the gemstones in it. You will then have the program print out a customized appraisal or gem identification report.

The beauty of the program is that if only a few of the stones characteristics are known, it will provide a list of all possible gemstones and prompt you for further information and testing. It will actually ask you questions such as, "Is the color banding curved, straight, or none noted?"

The workbench will be linked to the diamond catalog

section (see below) of the I.J.P. so that a record will be kept on all major gemstones and diamonds in stock.

Have you ever purchased a large parcel of diamonds? Did you ever wonder if you were getting the best value for the money? The workbench will evaluate a sample of stones from a parcel, give a breakdown of the average weight, price per carat, and quality of stones in the parcel. On top of this, it will give a statistical break down of the parcel. It will compute its own recommended price per carat for the parcel and also show you how much over or under the current wholesale prices each diamond is. This will certainly make buying mixed parcels much easier.

Of course, this program is a few years away. But when it arrives, it will be another powerful tool the jeweler will use in his daily work.

THE DIAMOND CATALOG SEGMENT

Largely, the jeweler's business is selling -- selling colored stones, diamonds, watches, and gold jewelry. Each diamond has its own fingerprint, its own characteristics. Whether the diamond costs $500 or $100,000, it is a large investment, at first for you and later the customer.

Now most jewelers rely on a manual record keeping method for controlling diamond inventories. Owing in large part to the Gemological Institute of America, you can catalogue diamonds into four distinct categories: color, clarity, cut, and carat weight. Also, the diamond can be diagrammed, its proportions measured, and its dimensions scaled. In short, you have the tools to categorize each of your diamonds.

Most gemologists will agree that diamond grading is partly guess work. Even well known gemological laboratories have been known to twice grade the same diamond differently. Nevertheless, in the United States, a highly trained following of jewelers and gemologists use the Gemological Institute of America's diamond grading system. In addition, the Gemological Research Corporation, San Mateo, CA, has developed an optical, computerized diamond grading system, based on the GIA grading system, which reportedly removes much of the guess work from diamond grading. Even colored stone grading systems have become available that will standardize the grading and evaluation of colored stones.

In the I.J.P., you will be able to list each diamond's exact specifications using the latest in gemological grading techniques. After appraising a diamond, you will store the information on your computer. Because computers and printers will be able to print high resolution graphics, you will, in entering the description of the diamond, have the tools to create a detailed image of the diamond, including a side, crown, and 3-Dimensional view. When all inclusions and surface characteristics are added, the image will even be shaded the proper color. Once this information is stored in the computer, you will have a permanent record of the diamond -- a diamond catalogue (a specialized section of the Inventory Control segment).

Along with the diamond's characteristics, current diamond values will also be catalogued. For example, many jewelers use the Rapaport Report to find diamond prices. Before this and other diamond price reports were made available, you had no simple way to know if you had bought diamonds wisely. In the I.J.P., you will download a similar price report into your computer; the pricing information will be directly received into the diamond catalogue, providing an instant means of repricing your diamonds.

How will this work? By linking prices with the qualities and sizes, the I.J.P. will instantly compute the current values of all the diamonds in your computer catalogue. As in many spreadsheet programs, which are covered earlier in this text, prices in the diamond catalogue will be automatically recomputed both at cost and retail using, of course, your designated markup.

A special section of the catalogue, called the Gemologist's Workbench will be used to create an appraisal data base of customers' jewelry. Until colored stone

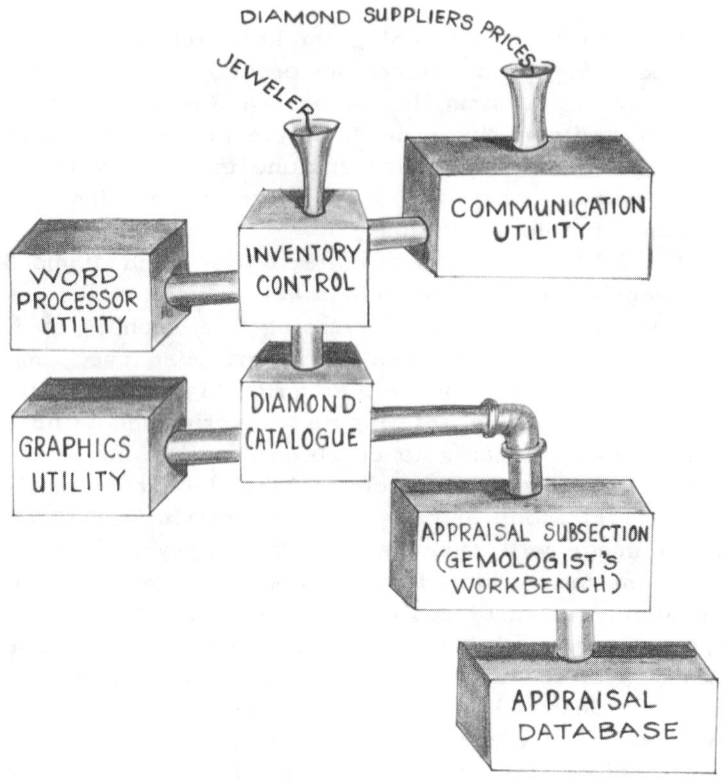

THE GEMOLOGIST'S WORKBENCH

Figure 2.14.1

grading becomes standardized and pricing more accurate, the appraisal sub-section will automatically compute diamond jewelry only--although it will allow for the manual input of prices, sizes, and sketches of colored stones. In addition to the diamond catalogue and pricing capabilities of this segment of the I.J.P., you will be able to enter information regarding the quality and weight of precious metals. Included with this will be a description of the jewelry. Tied in to the Word Processor program of the I.J.P., the program will then generate an appraisal and a diagram of the major diamonds in the jewelry. Now that you have a complete record of these diamonds you can print out -- at any time -- an appraisal including a detailed diagram.

The Computer-Aided Jewelry Design Program

Have you ever seen a computer aided design program produce a drawing of an object? Architects and designers

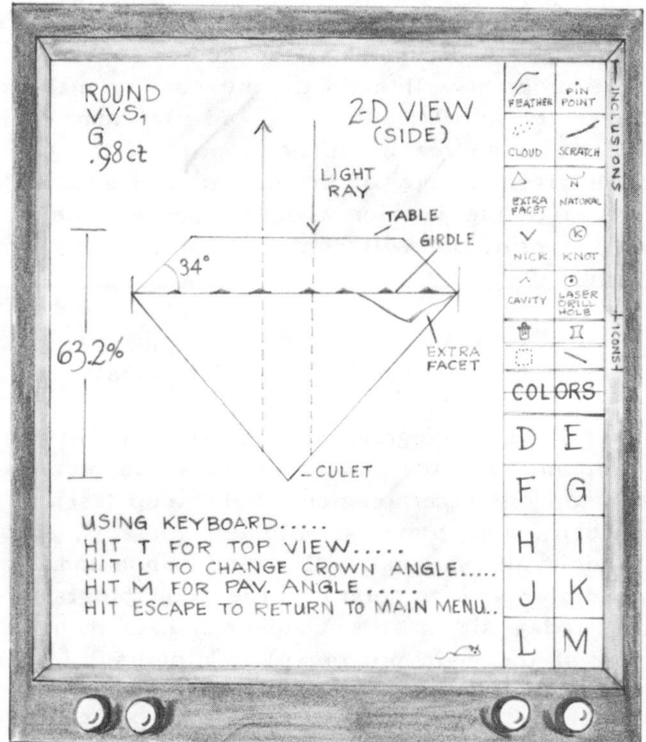

USEFUL FOR APPRAISALS AND FOR DIAMOND DEMONSTRATIONS FOR BOTH EMPLOYEES AND CUSTOMERS

Figure 2.14.2

have been using computers for years to design their products. Why couldn't the I.J.P include a computer aided jewelry design program?

The program will be similar to the 3-D diamond demonstration program of the I.J.P. Taking advantage of the speed of the computers processor and the high resolution color graphics of the computer, you could design a ring, pendant, bracelet, or other item of jewelry before the customer's very own eyes. The program will prompt your for pre-drawn parts of jewelry that you will overlay on each other until you had a composite picture of the item.

Additionally, you will take input from the customer by adding or subtracting various component parts of the jewelry until you had just what the customer wanted. Further, the program will estimate the cost to make the piece of jewelry in 10k, 14k, 18k, and platinum. With the use of a a high resolution color printer, the customer will be given a copy of the design and another copy will be given to the jeweler who will perform the work. Of course the print out will contain your company's name and address.

THE DESKTOP ORGANIZING PROGRAM

No Ideal Jewelry Program will be complete without a desk top organizer. And what is a desk top organizer? Most desk top organizer programs help keep track of telephone numbers, appointments, notes-to-yourself, and calendars. Additionally, most will include an automatic telephone dialer and calculator. The good programs on the market today sit in an unused portion of memory out of the way of the main program(s) in progress, ie. payroll.

When needed, you push one or two buttons and these programs spring into action. If the phone rings and you have to make an appointment, call up the desk top program and enter the information into your appointment calendar. You wanted to jot down a few notes, call up the notepad part of the organizer. When your done with it, hit a button and put it away. Did you need to tell a client what 10% off the signet ring is that she wanted for her husband -- call up the calculator.

These programs do not interfere with the program in progress. They are there when you need them but otherwise are a silent partner.

THE PROJECT PLANNER PROGRAM

The need to control the many, sometimes critical, phases of building ships is what led the United States Navy to develop a method of project management in wide use today. These methods employ the use of charts, either Ghant or PERT, to control the course of projects, large and small. Several good programs exist today that employ these methods -- programs that you can use to plot your yearly promotion, advertising, and vacation schedules.

These programs insure that those steps considered critical are completed before the next phase can continue. They let you see at a glance the entire year. If there is a vacation conflict or overlapping vendors or a promotion held while your scheduled to go to the July jewelry show, you will see it and be able to make the changes.

Sure, all of this can be done without the computer. But it is the interactive way in which these programs work that makes them so valuable. Annual planning that took days of time or wasn't done before will now be done in a fraction of the time. All these programs offer reports that allow you to look at this planning information in novel and different ways.

Annual planning is not the only "project" these programs will handle. What about the annual gem show or the opening of a new store? Letting your imagination run freely, these programs will prove a valuable aid in your effort to make your administrative chores flow smoother and more quickly.

THE LASER PRINTER

Here is a printer that is quiet, prints over 6 pages per minute on almost any kind of paper with a near type-set quality look. Why will you need a printer like this?

The laser printer is a workhorse -- reliable and powerful. With this printer, using the word processor in the I.J.P., you can write a personalized typewritten letter to over 2,000 customers in about 4 hours. Of course, you have to sign, fold, insert, lick and stamp all of these, too. Imagine. You can now send out a small jewelry newsletter. Your salespeople can send personal letters to their customers. And, all your correspondence will have that "polished" look.

Do you need to prepare an employee manual or an annual report? With the Laser printer you no longer have to send these out to be typeset; you will have your own typesetter in your store. With the proper software to drive the laser printer, it will be able to create camera ready black and white copy for newspaper advertising.

Does the laser printer sound too good to be true? This book was typeset on a laser printer using an IBM PC.

Summary

These programs and equipment along with the remainder of the I.J.P. will be combined to create a powerhouse for you. Everything that is contained in the I.J.P. can be done manually but the I.J.P will be an extra ally -- an ally that will take time to learn its full breadth -- but one that will be well worth getting to know.

The above productivity tools, a few that exist now and others that will exist in time, are only a sample of what is yet to come. Take your time to savor, question, learn, and grow like the rings on the pond.

15

AN OVERVIEW OF THE I.J.P.

This concludes the I.J.P. segments. You may have noticed a common thread running throughout all the segments -- features (like English like query language and security) that showed up again and again. Many of these segments, as yet, do not exist in the whole. Maybe someone is writing it now and, if they are, I hope that they will have read these and the following chapters. Programs that do exist may have additional features that are not presented in these chapters, but if you regard the I.J.P. as a foundation of knowledge from which you will grow in understanding of computers and your business -- than the I.J.P. will have served its purpose. I know that as you get started or as you mature in the use of computers as a tool for profit and as a tool for productivity that you will dream up many uses for the computer in your business.

A few programs that are now available do have many of the same functions as shown in the I.J.P. Supermicrocomputers, such as the AT&T 3B, the IBM AT, and the Apple 32 bit series, are within your reach. These supermicrocomputers use 16- and 32- bit microprocessors, have millions of bytes of Random Access Read-Write Memory (RAM), and the potential for gigabytes (billions--enough to hold entire encyclopedias and more) of disk storage. They are capable of doing many processes at one time (multi-tasking); they are user-friendly; and they will change the way we do business today. For the most part, they use a portable operating system (UNIX or XENIX) or a standard operating system (MS DOS), which enable programmers to port their programs to these machines with a minimum of reprogramming effort.

The I.J.P. will be a series of portable program written for these machines. Consisting of the most sophisticated and advanced features, such as windows, mice, optical scanners, laser printers, high speed modems, the I.J.P. will evolve. It will be created by the demands of the market place, created by your need to compete in the business environment of the 1980's, 1990's, and beyond the second ring.

The computer will not be the only answer for you, but if you are not only to stay in business but to make a profit and grow, then you should keep sight of the basics -- those of service, reputation, quality, and expertise. And you will learn to use computers in the information age, to . . . .

-- keep track of your customers, your employees, your potential customers, your suppliers, your appraisals, your inventory, and more.

-- teach yourself, your customers, and your employees.

-- communicate in the global marketplace that is evolving around you.

-- be more productive in the everyday chores you now do.

Why consider the computer as a marketing tool? Marketing is focusing the energy of your firm to the customer who is most likely to buy the services and goods you offer. Those of you who learn to control information, will control your market and your profit, and what better tool can control information than the computer?

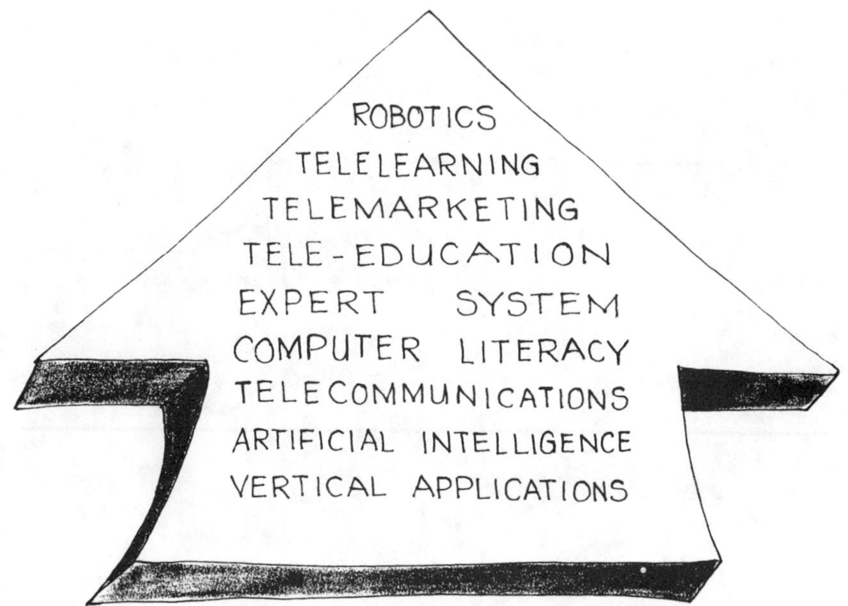

FUTURE USES OF COMPUTERS

Figure 2.15.1

- PART 3 -

COMPUTERS -- LANGUAGES, HISTORY, AND TRENDS

1

OPERATING SYSTEMS AND LANGUAGES

DISCUSSION OF TERMS

ASSEMBLY LANGUAGE--A language composed of mnemonic symbols that are later converted to machine language. It frees the programmer from having to worry about memory addresses or locations. Assembly language is the language of choice when speed is the only consideration. Assembly language programs are machine dependent in that they will not run without major modification on other types of microprocessors.

BINARY CODE--Or machine language--Code made up of two different values assigned to each code element.

BITS--Binary digit-abbreviated. Meaning one of two values (on-off) (1-0) (yes/no).

BYTE--Means eight bits used as a unit, it can be two numbers and one character.

COMPILER--A low level program that generates a machine language program from a high level language.

CONCURRENCY--Another term for multi-tasking, performing more than one job at a time.

MACHINE DEPENDENCE--Program that only works on one machine or microprocessor. Program must be rewritten to run on another machine.

PORTABILITY--Ability of a program or operating system to be used on more than one type of computer without major revision. Programs must be written with portability in mind otherwise a program written in a portable language may not be as portable as one might think. "C" language and Modula 2 are examples of portable languages and UNIX is an example of a portable operating system, which was written mostly in the "C" language.

PORTING--Changing over to another computer, ie. Port a program (so that it will run) from this computer brand to an other computer brand. This term is most frequently used in conjunction with adapting software to run on another type of computer. The act of porting usually requires a change in the source code of a program.

PRINT SPOOLING--Allows a file, which is temporarily loaded into RAM, to be printed while performing other functions on the computer.

You may already know that a computer program is a set of properly arranged bits and bytes (on-off signals), called binary code or machine language, that the computer microprocessor understands and translates into understandable and useful operations. Programmers write programs in computer languages. Computer language, which come in three categories--Low, Medium and High level --

are, for the most part, translated into binary code by the operating system of the computer or by a special program called a compiler, which runs under the guidance of the operating system.

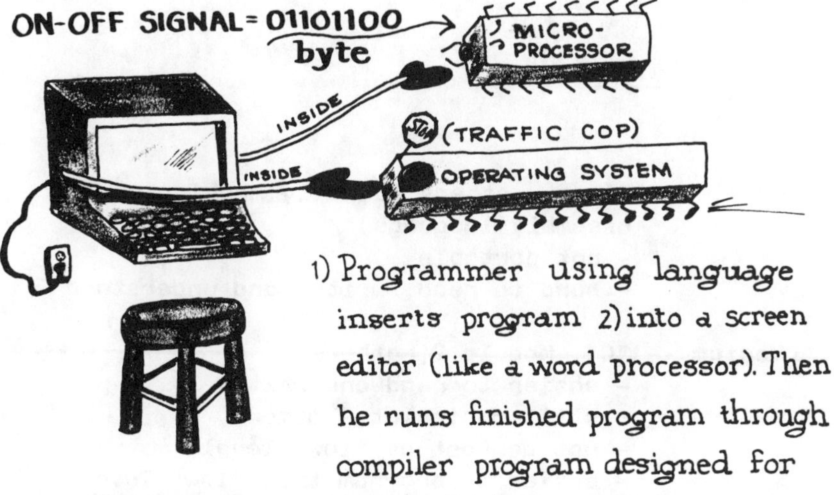

STEPS USED TO PRODUCE
A WORKING PROGRAM

Figure 3.1.1

You would find it most uncomfortable to think in machine language. So computer scientists have devised computer languages to talk with the computers. Because the computer must use its microprocessor to translate high level languages (the easiest computer languages for the human to understand) into binary data, they are generally the slowest of the three levels of computer languages.

```
LOW    -- Binary, others (usually machine or
          assembly language)
          - not portable
          - hard to read, write, and understand

Medium -- "C", Modula 2, others
          - easier to read and write
          - still manipulates memory
          - not as fast as "low" level
          - easier to program than "low" level
          - most portable

High   -- COBAL, FORTRAN (Primariliy mini- and
          mainframe), BASIC, PASCAL (Primarily
          microcomputers), ADA (Dept. of Defense),
          others
          - run slower than machine or "C"
          - easiest to write & understand
          - not as portable as medium level
```

THREE LEVELS OF LANGUAGES

Table 3.1.1

Since the quickest route between two points is a straight line, the languages that speak closest to the level of the microprocessor, the low level language, will be understood most quickly by the microprocessor. The computer language that speaks closest to the computer is again called machine language (the inventor of this term probably felt as though this was apt to describe what the language does: it speaks the machine's language). Machine language programs are the fastest running programs; however, they can only be used on the microprocessor for which they were originally written. Since different microprocessors have different electronic paths that they devote to processing, machine language programs cannot be carried over to other computers. Only if the computer has the same central microprocessor can the program be ported to (used in) another computer. Lastly, to program in machine language, a very difficult project, the programmer must know what electronic paths his computer's microprocessor uses.

A language that lies between Medium level and machine language is Assembly language; instead of binary code, it uses a pseudo-code. So in a sense, it, too, needs to be compiled into binary code, just like higher level languages.

To avoid rewriting Assembly language programs, they should be run on one type of microprocessor; if the programmer changes to another microprocessor, the Assembly language program will have to be rewritten for the new microprocessor -- this is called machine dependence. Assembly language is easier to use than machine language, but harder to use than high level languages. Today's programmers do very little machine language programming; almost all applications that require high speed processing are done in Assembly language. In practice, it is nearly as fast as machine language but much easier to use.

High level languages, as we recall, are easier for humans to grasp, but run much slower on computers than machine language because of the extra processing muscle needed to convert them to machine language. High level languages are similar amongst computers that use different microprocessors. For them to run on a microprocessor they must be compiled into machine language; high level language compilers do exist for computers with many different microprocessors. In theory, people can learn one or two languages and implement them on most computers (although, in practice, most high level languages are still machine dependent -- only to a much lesser degree than machine language). Programmers develop applications faster in high level languages because the computer does most of the work. Only when a program needs to run extremely fast does a program need to be written in Assembly languages, and only in sections of the program's code in which the program seems to spend most of its time -- this speeds up the bottlenecks.

One of several high level languages used today by serious programmers is "C" language, a Medium level language. "C" language (yes, it needs a compiler , too) is one of the very few languages that can be ported from computer to computer with little or no modifications (MODULA 2 is another one). "C" offers a combination of qualities that are present in both machine language and high level languages. It is becoming a popular microcomputer and minicomputer language.

Ideally, a program should only have to be written once. As long as the program was written in a high level language, you should be able to run Brand X's computer program on Brand Y's computer; yet for the most part programs must be recoded (meaning rewritten) for the new computer. Why?

The major reason is that most languages have syntax rules that tell the computer how to use monitors, disk drives, printers, modems and so forth (these devices are commonly called input/output devices or I/O devices). Because the microprocessors of many brands of computers do vary, so is the way that the languages treat these I/O devices. For those languages that address these devices directly in the main syntax of their languages, they have to be modified before they can be ported to another computer. The languages that can move freely from one computer to another are those that do not directly address these I/O devices but rather leave that to the compiler of the machine to which it is being ported. Once a computer manufacturer has written a compiler for his computer for a portable language (ie. "C" language) any program written in that language can be run on that machine.

Portability is an illusive concept. Varying degrees of portability exist among computer languages. For example, high level languages are generally more portable than low level language, but significant modifications may still have to be made to a program written in a high level language. "C" language is on the highest plateau of the portability spectrum -- it may even need slight modifications, especially when being ported to a sharply contrasting microprocessor than the one for which the "C" language program was originally written.

Here is the essence of portability. If you have just paid a programmer $10,000 to develop a machine language program for your Brand X computer, and if you decide to sell the program to defray your costs, you will have to sell other jewelers your Brand X computer or re-write your program to work on their computers, which defeats your original intentions. In either case, rewriting the program costs additional money. Thus, if a programmer writes an application in a portable language such as "C", his cost of rewriting it is greatly reduced, and it will also run on a greater variety of microprocessors.

Operating Systems

The first true operating system was developed by IBM in 1964: called the operating system (OS)/360. It cost over $400 million to develop.

What is an operating system? An operating system is a low level language program, usually written in Assembly language, that carries out the commands of the user and the commands of the program in progress.

For example, in the AR segment of the Ideal Jewelry Program, you and the program interact with each other and the operating system, which in turn gives the computer commands to carry out the programmed tasks. The operating system is, with rare exception, always present within the computer's Random Access Read-Write Memory (RAM), but it is usually invisible. The first job of the operating system is to standardize the way in which the computer's resources (ie. the I/O devices) are made available to you and the programs in progress. The operating system is in a sense the computer's traffic cop, acting as the go-between among the computer, hardware, software, and you. The operating system directs all the bits and bytes (on-off signals) that the microprocessor needs in order to make the program, disk drives, modems, printers, and keyboards work correctly. Several different operating systems can work on one computer, some at the same time. Remember, however, that each brand of computer usually has only one microprocessor, and therefore can only run programs that have been compiled for that one microprocessor.

For an operating system to work on a particular computer it must directly address the microprocessor in that computer. Keep in mind that most operating systems are written in a low level language. Since all computers have operating systems, and since most computers have several operating systems that can run on their brand of microprocessor, all a computer has to do to understand a program is to have an operating system capable of understanding the language in which that particular program is written.

Some operating systems perform one task at a time. For example, it will print a letter, view a database, and then manipulate a spreadsheet program, in that order: this is called single-tasking. Other operating systems will do more than one job at a time: this is called multi-tasking or concurrency. Most microprocessors are fast and spend most of their time waiting. To make use of this waiting time, the multi-tasking operating system switches quickly back and forth among jobs, giving the impression of doing more than one job at a time.

Another important task of the operating system is to provide a set of standardized rules for the transfer of data from hardware to software. This is especially evident when the computer has to transfer bits and bytes from the computer's RAM to the computer's disk drives. This is a very complicated job. The operating system hides the nuts and bolts from the user; to him it is simply pushing a few buttons on the keyboard. Lastly, the operating system guards against errors. If the user makes an entry error on the keyboard the operating system will catch him, tell him, and offer him a chance to correct the problem.

One important example of concurrency that comes in handy is print spooling. Print spooling, for example, lets you print a letter at the same time your bookkeeper posts the Accounts Receivables. Because it frees the computer to perform other tasks while the printer is printing, this is a valuable feature.

Portability

Until now you may have wondered why the discussion turned to computer nuts and bolts. Understanding how computers, operating systems, languages, programs, and portability relate is important information -- if you are deciding on computerizing your business, it could literally save you thousands of dollars.

What is the significance of language and operating system portability? The advice most computer consultants used to give to prospective clients in choosing a computer system for the first time was to choose the software first and then the system. The reason, of course, is now obvious. Most of the software that has been written for jewelers has been written in a language that is dependent on one specific brand of microprocessor. You can pick your computer first and be limited by your software choices or you can pick the software and be limited by the choice of computers.

Only recently has the concept of Portability ripened to significance. Historically, most computer manufacturers wanted to keep their operating systems, programs, and computers propriety: only they could service them. A portable program, on the other hand, would work on a number of computers (remember -- this depends on a compiler for that language being available for that machine), giving you a much wider choice of computers from which to choose and most importantly, giving you the ability to upgrade computers, at the same time continuing to use the same program.

Microprocessors

As you may have guessed, each microprocessor and, therefore, each computer, has its own strengths and weaknesses. For example, the microprocessor used in the IBM PC is faster and and more capable than the microprocessor in the Apple IIE; the microprocessor in the IBM System 36 minicomputer is faster than the one in the IBM PC. Each program relies heavily on the capabilities of the computer for which it was written. Because more powerful microprocessors are capable of handling more data in memory, programs can be more sophisticated. This enables the programmer to develop programs that serve the needs of the jeweler much more adequately. In brief, the more powerful the microprocessor the more respectable the programs can be. This, however, does not mean that programs written for less powerful computers are not competent. It only means that these programs have to work harder to produce the same results than a more powerful microprocessor. For example, you might have to wait longer for the monitor to refresh or you may find that the program cannot store adequate amount of data on one storage device such as a floppy disk drive.

What about the less than portable jewelry programs available today? Aren't they good enough to suit your needs? Yes. In fact, they represent the field of programs available to you today. Until programmers write portable programs, the jeweler will continue to choose the software before the hardware, and loose portability and access to a broad base of software.

Today, computers and operating systems are powerful and capable of running portable, multi-tasking, multi-user operating systems, languages, and programs. When jewelry retailing programs are written for these computers, they too will be powerful and portable from computer to computer. When that time comes, every jeweler who wants a computer should get one.

2

THE TRENDS

DISCUSSION OF TERMS

MOUSE--A mechanical or optical pointing device used to move the cursor about the computer display. It's name comes from its shape: it is designed to fit the hand comfortably. Some programs and operating systems make special use of the mouse, ie. the Apple "MacIntosh" line of computers.

It is interesting to note that two of world's seven largest corporations are beginning to be inexorably tied to the jewelry business: DeBeers gave us the diamond, and IBM the computer. Both firms have created the demand for their products through sound marketing techniques. The diamond, on the one hand, is the jeweler's lifeblood; the computer, on the other, paves the path to greater profits and productivity. For all of us, this writes a lesson in granite: marketing is the key to profits.

Before talking more bits and bytes, let's look at how IBM does it. IBM has never laid off, never unionized, and never failed to make a profit. Most of the success of IBM can be traced to Thomas Watson, Sr. He believed strongly that Research and Development was the key to growth, that a company should offer job security, constantly retrain its employees, hire from within, and put the company above departmental loyalty. Further, he believed a company should hire bright, aggressive, and persistent people, and they should be rewarded for good performance. IBM seems never to have lost sight of the basics: the salesman has to sell himself first and give the customer the service and support he deserves. Thomas Watson said it all here--that real success in a firm comes when the firm brings out the best in its people.

To understand how computers can help the jeweler, let's step back a minute and look at the history of computers and how they travelled from the past to the present. Of course, to talk of computers we should talk about IBM, but first, let's again look at IBM as a company. Of all the corporations started at the turn of the century, IBM remains intact from its foundation; others survived but not as the same company. In 1982, IBM owned 11,000 patents and spent over $3 billion on Research and Development (R&D). Its founder, Dr. Herman Hollerith, started the company in 1896 and called it the Computer-Tabulating-Recording Company. In 1914, Thomas Watson, Sr. joined the company, soon became the General Manager, and in 1924 changed the name to its present form, International Business Machines (IBM). Watson saw the company through the pre-computer era, until his son, Thomas Jr., took over and led the way to the line of computer products the company now sells.

Part of the R&D funds IBM spent in 1940 was for the MARK I computer. This was the first computer developed by IBM; they did not market it. In 1951, the Remington Rand company developed the UNIVAC computer; this was the first commercially available computer. Its name became a household word. When people thought about computers, they thought about UNIVAC. These were beastly computers. Taking up rooms of space, weighing tons, and water cooled, these behemoths required an army of technicians and programmers to run. They constantly broke down and consumed megawatts of power. The invention of the vacuum tube, by Sylvania, made these computers possible. Before they were even marketed, however, Bell Laboratory had invented the transistor--in 1946, but it wasn't until 1959 that we saw the first transistorized computers on the market.

By the late fifties IBM had regained its lead in the computer market, and by 1961 IBM was larger than its seven major competitors (see figure 3.2.1).

These firms concentrated on filling voids that IBM had left in the market place, a trend that continues through today.

Sperry-Rand
Control Data Corporation
Honeywell
Burroughs
National Cash Register
Radio Corporation of America
General Electric

SEVEN MAJOR IBM COMPETITORS IN 1950'S

Figure 3.2.1

In 1964, IBM developed the closed architecture 360 series computers ("closed" means that propriety or hardware and software support was available only from IBM). The 360 offered a new concept: upward software compatibility. Software developed for the 360 worked on successive computers (these programs would not, however, work on any computer other than an IBM). The 360 and its younger brother, the 370, were large computer systems.

IBM concentrated on the larger systems through the 60's and 70's. This again left a void for the other firms to fill. To fill this void, many companies including Digital Equipment Corporation, Burroughs, and other developed the minicomputer. This signalled the gradual development of smaller and less expensive (than mainframes) computers that would later evolve into the desktop computer we know today (you can see the vast change of philosophy through which IBM went in order to develop their line of of a personal computers, for theirs was a mainframe computer mentality. It is because of IBM's name that desk top computers are today considered a serious business tool; it is because of the voids left by IBM in the personal computer peripheral and software market place that has brought the plethora of third party software and IBM compatible computers).

About this time, AT&T developed the UNIX operating system to run on the Digital Equipment Corporation's (DEC) PDP series of computers. Again, upward compatibility and, for the first time, "portability" became a buzzword. At first the UNIX operating system was written in machine language on the PDP-9 (an older model minicomputer made by Digital Equipment Corporation). Dennis Ritchie, a programmer at Bell Laboratories (who decided that, when changing computers, there had to be a better way than to constantly rewrite programs) developed the "C" language. It followed the "B" computer language. Ritchie developed "C" to be portable from one microprocessor to another. To put it to the test, he rewrote the UNIX operating system in "C". Now UNIX is available on a greater variety of computers, from microcomputer to mainframe, than any other operating system. Today UNIX and "C" offer the greatest portability of any operating system and computer language.

The Intel Corporation and other microprocessor manufacturers kept reducing the size and increasing the power of microprocessors. The year 1974 saw the Micro-Instruments Telemetry Systems (MITS) ALTAIR 8800 microcomputer. Its cost was $400; they sold 1,500 computers. In 1977, the Tandy Corporation began marketing the Radio Shack Model 1 computer. Not until the Apple computer and Visicalc hit the street in 1979 did the microcomputer hit a grand slam: it was the universal acceptance of the electronic spreadsheet and the Apple computer that saw the widespread acceptance of the microcomputer as a business tool. In 1979, Apple, Radio Shack, Commodore, BASF, and Verbatim shared over $140 million in sales.

Now we have the tried and true mainframe computer market, the intermediate minicomputer market, and the exploding microcomputer market. As we read this, the distinction between minicomputer and microcomputer fades to "supermicrocomputer."

IBM saw the potential in the microcomputer market. In July, 1980, IBM created an Independent Business Unit, the Entry Systems Division in Boca Raton, FL. IBM gave the Entry Systems Division the task of designing and producing the IBM PC in one year's time. Within one month, the team, headed by Don Estridge, submitted the design to IBM for approval; on August 15, 1981, the IBM PC was introduced to the public. In the years since the IBM PC's introduction, it has gone from a zero share of the microcomputer market to become the predominant microcomputer standard on the market today. Before 1986, more IBM PC's and compatibles will have been produced than any other computer in history. By virtue of numbers it is the standard in personal computers. More than forty other IBM computers, taunting IBM PC compatibility, have been brought to market. Most claim to have faster and more powerful processors and enhanced features that the original IBM PC did not have. Figure 3.2.2 lists the companies that I know to manufacture IBM PC compatible computers.

IBM watched the market closely before jumping. They borrowed the open architecture concept from Apple Computer (Open architecture meant that IBM made the complete design details of the computer available to other manufacturers). IBM bought most of the computer's parts from outside manufacturers. For example, the disk drives allegedly came from Tandon or Control Data Corporation. They assembled the parts into IBM PC's at the Boca Raton plant, enabling IBM to keep the price of the computer within reach of most small businesses. Although the microprocessor and other components they used in the computer were not the latest, they were inexpensive and powerful. People knowing of IBM's reputation for service and quality saw in the IBM PC a serious computer, one that was worthy of their investment. At the time of its

ACT Ltd.
American Telephone & Telegraph
Articulate Computers
Bytec-Comterm
Canon USA Inc.
Colby Computer
Columbia Data Products
Compaq Computer Corp.
Compucorp
Corona Data Systems
Digigraphic Systems Corporation
Docutel-Olivetti Corporation
Durango Systems
Eagle Computer
Electro Design
Future Computers Ltd.
GRiD Systems Corporation
Gavilan Computer Corporation
International Business Machines
Intertec
JONOS International
Leading Edge Products
Logical Business Machines
MAD Computer
Micro Craft Corporation
NEC Home Electronics
North Star Computers
OSM Computer Corporation
Olympia USA Inc
Otrona Advanced Systems Corporation
Panasonic
Polo Microsystems
Pronto Computers
Radio Shack/Tandy Corporation
STM Electronics
Seattle Computer
Seequa Computer Corporation
Sharp Electronics Corporation
Sperry Corporation
Stearns Computer Systems
Strategic Technologies
TAVA Corporation
TeleVideo Systems
Texas Instruments
Toshiba America
Visual Computer
Wyse Technology
Xerox

MANUFACTURERS OF IBM PC COMPATIBLE COMPUTERS
Figure 3.2.2

introduction, it answered a large need in the marketplace: the need for a serious, inexpensive business computer.

Software development for the IBM PC followed the computer's popularity. Now over 4,500 programs are available for the computer. Software companies even brought the UNIX operating system and the "C" language to the PC, making it the best supported, standardized computer on the market.

Apple and Xerox

Let's drop back several years to Xerox Corporation's Palo Alto Research Center (PARC) in California. There, researchers developed the Star computer work station. Although the computer did not sell in droves it claimed some of the most advanced programming technology of its time. Xerox brought us the mouse, icons, and windows. The mouse is a hand held device that replaces cursor keys on the computer keyboard. By sliding the device on a flat surface it controls a pointer on the screen by which the user can execute computer commands. The icons are symbols on the computer terminal much like the international "no smoking" signs we know today, ie., the red circle on a white background with a red hash mark over a cigarette. The icons are features that the computer operator uses to understand and execute simple commands.

Windows are multiple programs on the same monitor seen as overlapping tiles that can be expanded and contracted, removed, or placed on the top or on the bottom of the screen or each other. Imagine a deck of cards with the ace of spades on the bottom of the deck. Spread the cards out so that they overlap each other, remove the Ace of Spades from the bottom and place it on the top: windowing has the same effect on the screen.

In 1983 Apple Computer of Cupertino, California introduced the Lisa computer that used many of the same techniques as did the Xerox Star. In 1984, Apple introduced the MacIntosh computer. This again used the icons, windows, and mouse that had been developed years earlier. These three features enable a person unfamiliar with computers to quickly grasp simple operations, making the machine extremely easy to use.

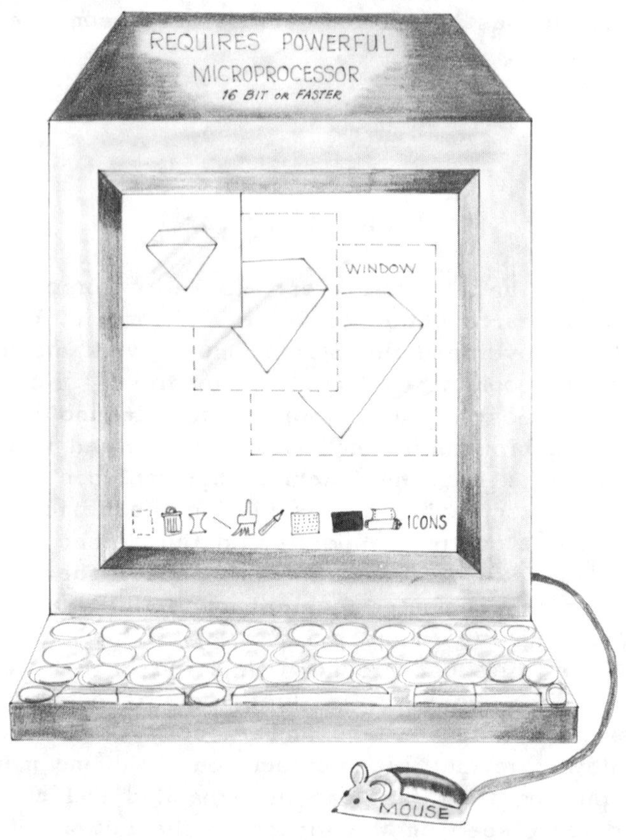

WINDOWS

Figure 3.2.3

Apple Computer was started in a garage by two people: Steve Jobs and Steve Wozniac. Wozniac, the engineer, brought us the Apple computer and Jobs, the entrepreneur, brought us the company -- the first company to make the Fortune 500 within 5 years. The Apple computer was developed using open architecture. This enabled outside vendors to make I/O devices and add-on peripherals for the computer, making a generic computer customized to the user's needs, much like what IBM did later. Today Apple produces one MacIntosh 32 bit computer every 7 seconds. They still market the Apple II line of computers and the MacIntosh line of computers. They recently announced the Apple 2C computer, with others soon to follow.

In January of 1984, the breakup of the AT&T company freed that giant from the reins of government control and AT&T now markets its own line of computers. Their line starts with the AT&T Personal Computer, which is an IBM PC compatible computer with a faster microprocessor than the IBM PC, and their line ends with a superminicomputer, which costs over $100,000. All but the Personal Computer are based on the UNIX System V operating system. The Personal Computer uses the same operating system as the IBM PC. Soon AT&T will announce a computer costing less than $6,000 with a hard disk drive that will compete directly with the IBM PC AT computer, which also has a hard disk drive. This new computer will probably run UNIX System V and a window of PC DOS, which is the IBM PC and AT operating system. That will mean that the user could run all the applications available to the IBM PC, and run the more powerful multi-user and multi-tasking, licensed UNIX operating system.

Radio Shack

The Tandy Corporation has about 8,000 stores under its wing. They sell a complete line of computers for home and business. They make an IBM PC compatible computer and as the top of their line, have a multi-user and multi-tasking computer that operates under the XENIX operating system, which is a version of UNIX. Tandy appears to have long range plans to keep themselves in the volatile computer market for years ahead.

Osborne Computer

In July of 1981, Osborne Computer shipped its first portable computer, about the same time IBM introduced their IBM PC. When other microcomputer manufacturers promised to have their computers out on time and didn't, Osborne computer did. Because of this, their third month of sales grossed over $1 million. Adam Osborne started the company and turned operation over to a Chief Executive Officer.

For a while Osborne Computer could do no wrong. But they had limited production and quality control experience, ran into shipment difficulties, and were forced to make recalls; in the spring of 1983, a company that had a $10 million line of credit with the Bank of America the year before, saw its first of several large million dollar losses. In 1984, the company was fighting bankruptcy. The Osborne Computer then started a trend toward power and portability in computers. Imagine carrying a computer on a trip or to a business meeting: Adam Osborne made this possible.

Compaq Computer

At last count 49 companies have developed computers riding the coattails of the IBM PC. One company stands out amongst all these: Compaq Computer. In 1983, three entrepreneurs started Compaq Computer Corporation. They saw a need to develop a portable IBM PC compatible computer that would be so compatible that it would run greater than 95% of the software that ran on the IBM PC. In their first year of sales Compaq computer grossed $111 million. The company is well run; they had a product that filled a need; and they brought it to the market on time through a network of well-established dealers -- usually the same dealers who carried the IBM PC. To stay ahead of the race, Compaq and many of the other companies following in IBM's footsteps are improving on the IBM design while still maintaining compatibility. For those companies who have become too compatible, they have felt the sting of IBM's legal department and have had to change their designs slightly, slowing down their sales.

Can you see how the development of computers, operating systems, and languages have led to the current state-of-the-art affairs? The computer industry is oozing at the seems. So much demand -- for information and expertise -- exist from users from all walks of life that the the computer industry is developing software, training aids and hardware at a frantic pace. Maybe, through your enriched understanding of how the the modern computer has evolved, you will be able to ask the right questions and see the "big picture" of computers and software and how they relate to the jewelry business.

3

WHAT DOES IT ALL MEAN?

DISCUSSION OF TERMS

ARTIFICIAL INTELLIGENCE--The ability of a computer to display functions thought of as connected with human intelligence. These are possible due to advance programming methods and may include self-correction, reasoning, learning, and an ability to improve functioning. It is also called heuristics. The primary languages that are used in artificial intelligence research include Prolog, Lisp, and Forth.

VERTICAL SOFTWARE--Programs written for one industry -- each containing features useful to that particular business or industry.

Democratization of Computers

What does this all mean to the jeweler? For years, only large companies could afford the mainframe computers and the army of systems analysts and programmers required to run them. Then came the minicomputer; all those companies that eyed the mainframe but couldn't afford it, bought a minicomputer. Still, the minicomputer was above the budget of most small businesses, so we saw the time-sharing services that are so familiar. "If I can't afford a computer, at least I could buy time on one," some of us said.

Now comes the microcomputer. While not nearly as powerful as the mini- or mainframe computers, it is, for most of us, adequate for our needs. Software for the microcomputer wasn't readily available at first; soon, though, thousand of applications evolved.

Software businesses sprang up, computer consultants began invading the yellow pages. "If there's not an application written for my needs, by golly, I'll have one developed. To defray my costs, I'll sell it to others...," was the general consensus. Soon programs were written for general applications such as word processing, and spreadsheets (this is called horizontal marketing). This left the vertical market, such as the jewelry business, the legal profession, the medical field, and the engineering fields, wide open for the entrepreneurial computer programmer.

Meanwhile, microcomputers became less costly while their processing power increased. Soon, what used to be the power of a minicomputer came to the jeweler in the form of a microcomputer at a fraction of its cost. Combined with the cost reduction, the increase in computing power, the advances in off-line storage devices such as laser disks and hard disk drives, and the widespread availability of other peripherals such as modems, printers, and alternate input devices other than keyboards and mice, computers have become democratized: the power of the few has fallen into the hands of the many.

Many people don't know how to best use this newfound freedom or aren't even aware of its presence, but it is there, nonetheless. The generic nature of the computer, to be everything to everybody, to fill the needs of the many, has put the computer in the middle of our lives.

Some modern thinkers profess that this is the most dramatic event in man's history. Perhaps a bit exaggerated, the development of microcomputers is a significant

NOT JUST FOR A SELECT FEW

Figure 3.3.1

event. Some of today's greatest thinkers are deeply involved in artificial intelligence (computers made to remember past experience and make decisions based on this experience). Their research will have a profound effect on us in years ahead, but where does that leave us now?

Jewelry related programs, sophisticated and inexpensive enough for the jeweler to use in his everyday business, are now starting to hit the market. For the programmer, this vertical market in the jewelry business is lucrative. Over 22,000 retail jewelry stores exist today, not to mention all the suppliers, manufacturers, and related professions. The programmer faces several problems in trying to reach these jewelers. First, each jeweler's business is different: Zales with over 1,200 stores, the "mom and pop" shop, and all the stores and chains between. It would be difficult to develop a program that is all things to all jewelers. Second, with the large number of available computers, multitude of operating systems and languages, deciding which to choose is a difficult decision. If the programmer picks the wrong ones, he will limit his market and his income.

Some jewelers will need a multi-user and multi-tasking computer with many terminals. Other jewelers will only need a single-user and single-tasking (does only one job at a time) computer. Owing to their larger volumes and multiple store locations, a few jewelers will need main-frame computers. And yet others will find networking of microcomputers to be a viable solution. For both the jeweler and the programmer, help is on the horizon. Although no one knows for sure when, IBM, AT&T, Apple Computer, and others are developing computers that will meet the future needs of many. These computers will be sold in basic models, be upgradeable, be upward compatible, use portable software, be powerful, and be within the price range of most jewelers. Here, now, are the MS DOS operating system standard in the microcomputer market and the UNIX operating system standard in the supermicro-computer and minicomputer market.

For programmers to write programs for the jeweler in other operating systems only serves the present, for the price of the software will not come down; the support of the programs, and the equipment will tie the jeweler to that program for years. To bring computing power within the reach of most jewelers, the programmer and jeweler should look to the future. A jeweler would be wise to seek a computer standard: upgradeable, powerful, compatible, and portable.

FREEWARE

What is the freeware concept? The value of the program is directly proportional to the benefits the program gives the user; that if it is useful, the user is asked to make a donation to the author. Like the Public Broadcasting System, which solicits donations from its viewers, freeware relies solely on the users to pay the program author for his work. The more useful a program, the greater the user base; the greater the user base, the greater the contributions.

In the public domain, several programmers have published programs that rival commercial products in their sophistication and arsenal of features. Although these programs are copyrighted and the authors do request a voluntary donation, they are free to the user. These programs cover communications, spreadsheets, data bases, word processing, and utility programs. In the future, freeware will expand to other areas as well. One software author has reportedly made over $500 thousand in donations for just one freeware data base program for the IBM PC and compatibles.

Some say that one in ten of those who use the programs donate to the author. Albeit a small number, as more of these programs begin to rival commercial products costing hundreds of dollars, more people will use these programs rather than those commercially available (This book was written with a freeware word processor).

4

UNIX "C" AND PC (MS) DOS

"C" Language

Earlier, we learned that "C" language came from "B" Language; Dennis Ritchie developed it to enable programs written in "C" to be moved from one computer to another. His efforts paid off. Today, many programmers choose to write programs in "C" so they won't have to rewrite the program for another brand of computer. For most, this saves thousands of hours of labor in program development and further broadens the program's potential market.

We also learned that UNIX was written in "C". When computer manufacturers bring a new computer to market, it takes developers about four to six months to develop a "C" compiler for that computer and six months to a year more to develop a UNIX operating system. Remember that in the early 1960's the development of the operating system (OS)/360 for the 360 IBM computer cost IBM over $400 million and took a team of experts many years. Even so, the OS/360 was a cumbersome and behemoth operating system.

Since "C" is a small language, it can be learned swiftly; its documentation is minimal. Further, "C" is a general purpose language that can be used to develop operating systems, data bases, word processors, and commercial programs. Lastly, "C" is a Medium level language, which means it is fast: programs written in "C" perform quickly.

Microsoft DOS (MS DOS) and Personal Computer DOS (PC DOS)

In 1981, the IBM PC arrived; with it came the PC DOS operating system, a special version of the Microsoft Disk operating system (MS DOS). MS DOS is the most widely used computer operating system -- over two million computers use MS DOS as their primary operating system. Almost all IBM PC and compatibles come with MS DOS (here we will treat PC DOS the same as MS DOS). Each new computer owner receives a limited or "User" license to run the computer with that operating system. This, by the way, is typical of most commercial software. If a company has more than one computer, for that company to legally use the same program on all the computers, the firm must buy a multiple-user license.

Although the IBM PC and compatibles are capable of running multi-user and multi-tasking operating systems, MS DOS and PC DOS are single-user and single-tasking. Some of those using the IBM and some of its compatibles with the more sophisticated operating systems, such as UNIX, claim that the computers perform more slowly than MS DOS. They say that the computer's microprocessor, the Intel 8088, is not fast enough to handle more than one user at a time. With the new generation of computers based on the Intel 8086 and 80286 microprocessors, IBM, AT&T, and other manufacturers are now producing multi-user and multi-tasking computers that perform much faster than the original IBM PC yet still are maintaining upward compatibility. Each jeweler should make his own choice based on seeing the computer configured (set up) in the manner that he requires.

When we look at UNIX and "C" Language as capable of running under the greatest variety of microprocessors, this makes them a standard; when we look at MS DOS running on the largest number of computers, this makes them a standard too. It is important to understand that most of the IBM PC compatibles use one of a family of microprocessors, the Intel 8088, whereas the UNIX operating system will run on virtually any 16 or 32 Bit microprocessor. So, how portable is MS DOS? Let us just say that while not as portable as UNIX, it does claim a lot of computers for which it is the main operating system.

Future versions of MS DOS will reportedly converge towards UNIX or a UNIX-like formula. The developments of UNIX, computers, and MS DOS will show a surprisingly similar evolution.

For example computers are becoming more powerful; so are the operating systems capable of using their power. The market place is beginning to display more and more sophisticated users -- people, in all fields, who two years ago never touched a computer but who today read computer magazines, belong to user groups, and who make daily, productive use of computers. These sophisticated users understand the concepts presented in this book; they are beginning to demand the power, the flexibility, and the growth of supermicrocomputers. So in short order, UNIX, MS DOS, users, and computers steer towards compatibility, portability, and standardization. Features that are good in the many will be brought together in the few. The operating system, the computer, and the user will grow to a new dimension that combines the old and the new.

What should the jeweler who needs a computer know about MS DOS and UNIX? MS and PC DOS are easier to learn than UNIX, but do not have the wealth of features that UNIX sports. Although with each successive revision of MS DOS, more and more UNIX like commands find their way into them. This matches the trend that shows microcomputers are turning into minicomputers or what we will call supermicrocomputers.

MS DOS is friendlier than most operating systems. Their error messages are clearer and more complete. Even so, to learn all the features of MS DOS requires hundreds of hours of trial-and-error. MS DOS is a healthy operating system that adequately shows the worth of the computers on which it was designed to run. The jeweler who determines he needs only one computer and who finds appropriate software that will fill his needs and run under MS DOS, will find that the IBM PC or its compatibles are a welcome business partner. If he needs a computer with more power than the IBM PC then he should look to the new generation of UNIX driven computers -- if he can find the software available to do what he wants.

UNIX--A ROBUST TOOL

UNIX, an AT&T operating system developed in 1970, is the only operating system that runs on the three categories of computers -- mainframes, minicomputers, and microcomputers. Over 200 companies offer over 1000 software packages that run under UNIX: these packages include word processors, spreadsheets, data base, accounting, and inventory control programs. A few of the programs were developed on early microcomputers then ported to UNIX; more often, the programs are highly sophisticated programs developed for use on mini- and mainframe computers then ported to UNIX. Industry insiders project that by 1986 UNIX related products will gross over $2 billion. Table 3.4.1 shows the versions of UNIX that AT&T has developed so far. Each is an improvement on the next.

AT&T offers two kinds of licenses for UNIX: a Binary or "User" license and a Source license. The "User" license is just what it says: a license to use the operating system. The Source license gives the buyer the right to adapt the code to specific needs and the right to resell it under a different name.

Twenty-one offspring of UNIX have been brought to market so far by holders of Source licenses. Of these, significant to microcomputer users is XENIX, a licensed supplier of a UNIX, adopted by the same supplier of MS and PC DOS, Microsoft of Bellevue, Washington. The MacIntosh

XL computer by Apple Corporation, the Radio Shack Model 16, and the IBM PC can all use XENIX. Also, nine UNIX-like operating systems, call them clones, have been developed by companies wanting to bring a similar product to the customer at a lower price (they don't have to pay royalties to AT&T -- these companies developed their systems from ground level using most of the features available in the licensed versions of UNIX.

SIXTH
SEVENTH
PWB/UNIX
SYSTEM III (1979)
SYSTEM V (1983)

UNIX PRODUCTS DEVELOPED BY AT&T

Table 3.4.1

When licensed vendors of UNIX port it to the microcomputer it may only be a multi-user or single-user version, but it will always be a multi-tasking version. Built of over 200 utility, business, and programming tools, it will easily tackle communications, electronic mail, file manipulation, word processing, text formatting, typesetting, accounting, graphics, and more. A programmer's workbench and a writer's workbench have both been developed for UNIX. Both of these offer their respective user a variety of useful tools. For the jeweler who doesn't like to look up misspelled words, that includes an on-line dictionary.

Compared to MS and PC DOS's, which required 250 kilobytes (250 thousand bytes) of disk storage, UNIX needs 8 megabytes (8 million bytes -- equals about 4,000 double spaced typewritten pages). With the drop in cost of hard disk drive systems for microcomputers, UNIX, although snug, will fit most hard disk configured systems. Critics of UNIX claim that its commands are cryptic, it is not easy to learn, it does not give good error messages, and, if the wrong command is given, it is easy to erase files. Proponents of UNIX claim that, although requiring a longer time to learn, once the user learns the system, its use becomes second nature: like driving a BMW -- designed around the driver.

More and more of the licensed UNIX vendors are producing an easy to learn, menu driven shell for UNIX, giving that layered effect discussed in the section on the Ideal Jewelry Program. Like an onion, on the surface this shell is easy to learn, tolerates errors well; underneath are even more powerful tools that will give the jeweler years of high power computing for his business. Indeed, the reason for UNIX's popularity is that it gives the user the tools to use the more powerful microprocessors on the market today. We could say UNIX is the minicomputer standard, whereas MS DOS is the microcomputer standard.

Since 1983, Digital Equipment Corporation (DEC), Data General, IBM, Hewlett-Packard, and AT&T have announced UNIX available for their mini- and superminicomputers. In April of 1984, IBM brought a licensed version of UNIX to market for the IBM PC, called UNIX/IX. Although only single-user, UNIX/IX is multi-tasking. The most powerful commercial computer in the world, the CRAY III, offers UNIX as its standard operating system. IBM and Amdahl both offer UNIX for their mainframe computers. Simply, UNIX is a general purpose operating system, portable, and easily customized to a company's needs. For programmers it makes their lives easier; for jewelers, it offers them flexibility and power that only 2 years ago would have cost 10 times more.

UNIX is not the only operating system that a jeweler can consider. Indeed, UNIX is not the easiest to learn, and usually requires more hardware to run (such as more disk storage and Random Access Read-Write Memory (RAM)). Programs for UNIX may tend to be more expensive than those written to run under DOS. UNIX does, however, offer a powerful standard the jeweler knows will be here for years ahead; it gives the jeweler three-tiered security, a layered operating system, an on-line help function and calculator, and electronic mail. UNIX is multi-tasking and usually multi-user. Should the jeweler decide to trade up to a more powerful UNIX operated computer, he will not have to retrain his staff on how to use the new operating system.

Because of the development of UNIX by AT&T, UNIX will play an integral role in the office of the future: AT&T now uses UNIX to control most of its telephone networks. Next UNIX will tie offices together with the PBX telephone network, offering a degree of service unknown today.

In summary, UNIX was developed by, backed by, and used by some of the biggest names in computers. It is the only operating system that crosses the boundaries of microcomputer, minicomputer, and mainframe computers alike. Although each jeweler should decide what is right for him -- because there are a lot choices -- UNIX deserves a close look.

UNIX IS SOLD BY IBM, AT&T, AND MANY OTHERS
IT IS ONLY OPERATING SYSTEM CAPABLE OF
RUNNING ON MAINFRAME, MINI, AND MICROCOMPUTER

Figure 3.4.2

5

LOCAL AREA NETWORKS

DISCUSSION OF TERMS

BATCH FILE--A special command for the computer to perform a series of predefined tasks without operator intervention; when combined with a timer function it will permit the computer to operate without an operator present. The batch file is called a shell script in the UNIX operating system.

ELECTRONIC MAIL--The replacement of inter- and intra-office paper correspondence through the use of computers and software specially designed to accommodate the greater throughput potential of electronic data.

FILE SERVER--A computer used in a Local Area Network (LAN) as the mother node. The file server usually contains a hard disk, printer, and other input/output (I/O) devices. It may or may not be able to be used as a stand alone computer while it acts as the network server.

Let's consider a hypothetical situation. Let's say that you've decided to buy a computer. You've found a software vendor with whom you are pleased. You like the programs; you've heard good things about them. The computer that the program runs on is the IBM AT or a compatible. You have 2 stores that are not in the same city, and desire a computer in each store. The program has a communications segment that enables the satellite store to download inventory, receipt, and sales information into the home office computer (by means of a specially designed command, called a batch file, the computer automatically does this every evening after the stores close). The jewelry programs that you have bought runs under MS DOS. Included with the computer is a hard disk drive, which can hold up to 20 million bytes of data (called 20 megabytes -- this equals about 10,000 double spaced typewritten pages), a dot-matrix printer, and a color, high resolution monitor.

After a few years you decide to put a computer on your desk and on your diamond sales counter. Because the system you chose is single-tasking and single-user, you must buy another IBM PC or compatible (so you can use the software you have already purchased) or you will be faced with having to sell the computer, and the software, with which you are already familiar, and buy a multi-user computer. Another option would be to change the operating system on the IBM PC to a multi-user system, such as UNIX, but, unless it operated a WINDOW of PC DOS, you would still be faced with the need to get a new software program. So, you choose another alternative: the Local Area Network (LAN).

With the LAN, you can tie together your two other computers to share your hard disk, your printer, and your modem. With the LAN, you share the hard disk drive on the bookkeeper's computer, and you avoid the expense of buying disk drives for your two new units. To make this work, you need only one special circuit card and cabling for each new computer. With the LAN software, you have data security, electronic mail, and continued use of the jewelry programs to which you have already grown accustomed. Deciding on a LAN, you saved yourself the trouble and expense of buying a multi-user computer or installing a new, and possibly expensive, different operating system and jewelry programs.

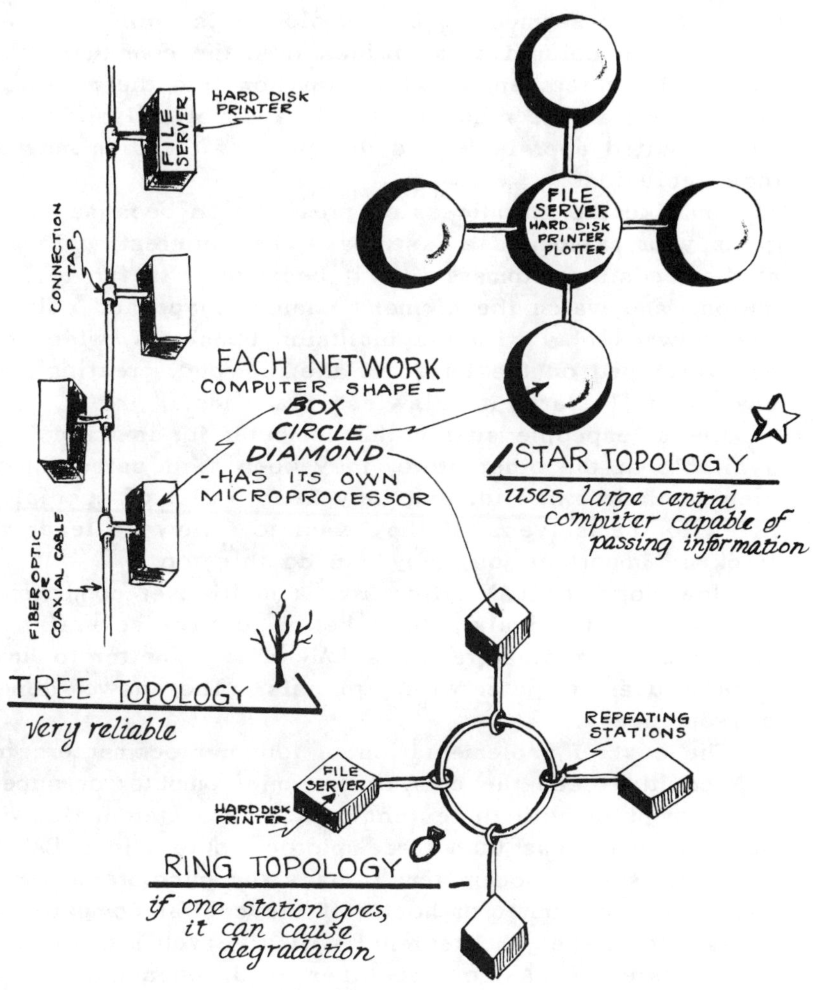

In simple terms, a LAN gives each computer in the network access to the same files. Since the selected LAN software does have security features, you are able to limit access to confidential files and still give the salespeople access to the 3-Dimensional diamond sales demonstration segment. The gemologist is able to extract diamond and colored stone prices from the computer. As needed, he enters appraisal information into the appraisal segment; at his request, it will automatically print out formatted appraisals and diagrams of the diamonds and their inclusions.

You like the graphic sales presentation because it gives your customers a fast, easy, and interesting look at diamonds. Customers like it because it is fun to push buttons and watch the diamond change shape and colors. They always play with the inclusion templates, which can be overlapped on the image of the diamond, creating images of I1 clarity to Flawless diamonds.

The salespeople search the computer for inventory available at the other store, they keep their sales figures in their own file, and they keep a list of special notes to themselves. If they want to follow up leads or track an important job, they can do this too.

How does the LAN differ from a multi-user computer with several terminals? Is it better to have several microcomputers clustered in a LAN or is it better to have a multi-user computer with terminals? The answer depends on your needs.

The cost of implementation of four microcomputers in a LAN could exceed the cost of one minicomputer or supermicrocomputer with three terminals. Three terminals will normally cost less than three microcomputers in a LAN. A terminal is not a computer; it uses the microprocessor of the central computer or host. If the central computer breaks down then the terminal will give you merely a blank stare. A LAN, on the other hand, when configured like a tree or star (as shown above) is quite reliable. For example, if a computer breaks down, the rest of the network will keep working. Also, some LAN software may not be able to accommodate updating the same database from different computers or the same file at the same time -- this could cause information loss. If the LAN software being used does not account for this, the computer will remember only the last updates.

In a multi-user system, the computer will always prevent two people from accessing the data at the same time. With a microcomputer, the you are free to download data from the file server (this is the computer with the hard disk) and manipulate that data in the manner you see fit. In the end, you should decide the best cost-to-performance ratio for your business. Before taking the plunge, you should look at the software available for the different machines, decide what you want, ask how long it will suit you, and how well the vendors will support it? With the LAN, you have many of the advantages of the minicomputer available to you. Too, if you go the way of a minicomputer or supermicrocomputer system, you can always use microcomputers as terminals.

– PART 4 –

WHERE ARE WE HEADED?

1

COMPUTER AIDED LEARNING

More than 50,000 students have passed the portholes of Gemological Institute of America training; this figure does not include those who have taken courses under the wings of the Gemmological Association of Great Britain, the Canadian Jewellry Institute and others. Many other institutes of secondary and higher learning include courses in jewelry making, design, gemology, and horology. For most of these schools, the past ten years have shown their greatest growth. Indeed, most of them pride themselves with the individual nature of their instruction. What would happen if these schools tied their home study students together into an Electronic Network?

Recently, Ron Gordon, the former Chief Executive Officer of Atari, formed the Electronic University. At last count they offered over 177 courses, all taught by accredited teachers and professors for college credit. The home study courses cost between $35.00 and $150.00. They range from math, science, law and finance, to anthropology and foreign languages. At specified times, the professor is available for a live chat with the students. From their homes the students can, via a modem and computer, and using special software provided by the University, register for courses, receive assignments, read a lecture, receive a message, and take a test. The student only has to dial a local Tymenet or Telenet number (like an 800 number) on his computer, he is then in touch with the school.

What are the advantages of tele-learning? For one, as tele-learning becomes available to the jewelry student, the cost and mailing time of assignments will be dramatically reduced (when I took the GIA Gemology courses in 1981, the average turnaround time for assignments was 12 days).

Secondly, the school's paper costs will be dramatically reduced -- the student could print the course work out on his printer. Third, although most instructors will be available by phone, by being available on-line at special hours the student could get special tutoring, ask questions, and receive feedback -- all of which adds an extra personal touch to the training. Fourth, the electronic mail feature, allowing the student to leave and receive messages at times when the instructor is not on-line, will speed other correspondence significantly.

Every student who enters the Massachusetts Institute of Technology is required to buy a computer. Carnegie-Mellon University is providing a network of IBM PC's throughout their campus so that every student has access to one. At Bradley University, the Engineering School is buying five or more IBM PC's per department and installing them in special laboratories for students use.

What does all this mean? College graduates in the years 1988 and beyond will be intimately familiar with programming and uses of computers. How does this affect the jewelry business? In several ways.

Many of the jewelry business's future leaders will come from schools with this computer awareness. Like the calculator, computers will be part of their everyday lives. The computer will extend their minds and make them capable of far greater productivity than is now thought possible -- not because they know more, or do more, but because the computer allows them to access the right information at the right time, and it allows them to reach beyond the corral of their own knowledge and rope the knowledge harnessed by the computer.

As computers begin to reach the jewelry schools, students and instructors will begin to depend on them. For example, now the student must look up charts for the information on refractive indices, specific gravity, and inclusions. Soon, programs will enable the gemologist to find the exact identification of gemstones merely by inputting data into a personal computer. Far-fetched? No. Reducing gemological knowledge to a set of rules the computer will remember, manipulate, and build on, although expensive and time consuming, is possible; this is called a Gemological Expert System and speaks of Artificial Intelligence (which is discussed in the next chapter). Jewelers who lack gemological training will be able to call upon their Gemology Expert program from their personal computer and get answers that will rival, if not outdo, the best gemologists.

The jewelry instructor will soon use the computer to tutor his students. What better way than a computer to show the four C's of the diamond?

Imagine a 3-Dimensional color view of a diamond. On the screen the student will see a large diamond with all its facets. It can be rotated in all directions, and the proportions adjusted to see the effect that a single beam of light passing through it will have on the brilliance. The student can adjust the table diameter, the pavilion depth percentage, the shape, the crown height, and the color, and can even lift predrawn inclusion templates and overlay inclusions onto the diamond's image. This will be similar to the way in which the FBI and other law enforcement agencies overlay facial features on a pad to create a composite sketch of a criminal.

At the sales counter, the salesperson could use the computer to do 2- or 3-Dimensional counter sketches. The sketches will be realistic, colorful, and well done. The salesperson could even obtain a print-out to give to the customer and to the jeweler for manufacture. The computer could even tell the salesperson the weight and the cost of manufacturing the jewelry.

Some might say, why bother? Why can't the jeweler continue with the time-proven methods he already has? He can, but service to the customer, raising that service to the highest possible degree, providing the customer with the best information he can is the jeweler's specialty? Aren't service and knowledge the largest competitive edges you have against mass merchandisers? The more professional you appear in the eyes of the public, the greater the chance of repeat and referral business. The technology is here today that will give you the tools with which you can better control your market. Will you use them?

In the classroom and on the sales floor, the computer will be used to teach more of what is commonly taught by the teacher and salesperson. The software used on the sales floor will be simpler and more entertaining; software used in the classroom will be more interactive, like a good coach, with more information given, but both will be effective conveyors of information.

For computer software developers, educational software is a big growth market. Is there any reason software like the above shouldn't be used to teach customers and jewelry students?

2

THE FIFTH GENERATION (Artificial Intelligence)

DISCUSSION OF TERMS

CAT-1--An expert system designed to help non-expert diesel repair people troubleshoot diesel engines.

EXPERT SYSTEMS--A thinking machine that has both the knowledge and intuition of an expert in a certain field. Heuristics is the study of artificial intelligence. Expert systems require a limited set of rules, a narrow field of knowledge, an audit trail, a means to learn from its mistakes, and a knowledge manager to work effectively with experts while developing the expert system. These programs are generally written in LISP, Prolog, or Forth.

INTERNIST/CADUCES--Expert system that examines 500 diseases and 3500 symptoms.

KNOWLEDGE MANAGERS--The developers of expert systems who extract knowledge from a professional and put it into a computer program. The knowledge manager attempts to break a field of knowledge down into a set of closely defined rules and inferences.

MYCIN--A medical expert system used by non-specialist doctors to detect and treat meningitis.

PARALLEL PROCESSING--In regard to Artificial Intelligence, refers to a process similar to that of the human brains ability to carry on more than one function at a time through the use of separate processors (separate portions of the brain), ie. walking and talking, breathing and knitting, day-dreaming and driving.

PUFF--A medical expert system on pulmonary disease.

To talk of Artificial Intelligence, three other topics have to be mentioned in the same breath -- the Japanese, the microprocessor, and computer language developments. Further, while you read about Artificial Intelligence (AI), imagine how Gemology could be reduced to a set of a few hundred rules and of how a computer could be programmed to be a Gemology Expert System. This may seem far-fetched and unrealistic; when you see the developments below, you, too, will know that this will be a reality.

What is Artificial Intelligence? AI is the ability of a computer to reason to a near human degree, the ability to learn from mistakes, the ability to interrelate data and logic, and the ability to infer. The major product of AI is Human Expert Systems: an Expert System is a thinking machine that has both the knowledge and the second sense of intuition of an expert in a given field (ie. doctors, lawyers, gemologists, and the rest).

Expert System developers, called knowledge managers, must sit with an expert in a given field, extract his knowledge, and put it into the computer. Through this interaction between computers and man, many narrowly defined fields of skill can be broken down into a set of facts and rules. The inference engine of the AI program will then use these rules to produce credible knowledge tools. For example Puff, a medical Expert system on pulmonary disease, has broken down that field into 50 rules. Mycin, another Medical Expert System designed to diagnose meningitis has been broken down into 450 rules and 1000 facts. The accuracy of diagnosis for these programs, although not 100%, is higher than that of 90% of those non-specialized doctors who use them.

A Geological Expert System, designed by SRI International Corporation to evaluate sites for mineral deposits, recently discovered a multi-million dollar deposit of rare ore. An Expert System called CAT-1 troubleshoots diesel engines. The Internist/Caduces Expert System at the University of Pittsburgh looks at 500 diseases and 3500 symptoms. To develop any such Expert System requires time, experience, and money.

An Expert System is most needed when the body of knowledge is available to a few and needed by many. It offers the non-expert the ability to make use of the years that a human expert has spent training. One thing is certain -- the larger the Expert System is, the more difficult it is to build and the more rules that are required to make it work. Most Expert Systems today cover fields narrow enough in scope that they will produce acceptable results. Because the Expert System will learn from mistakes and because the computer does not suffer from fatigue, often times it will give results that are better than those of a group of experts themselves.

AI requires computers with extremely powerful microprocessors. Some experts in AI say that at least 1 megabyte of RAM is the minimum required for significant AI work. Typically, major universities, such as MIT and UCLA, have conducted AI research

Besides a powerful microprocessor, a powerful language is needed to produce Expert Systems. The Japanese use Prolog; others are using LISP, which stands for List Processing. On microcomputers, Forth is also being used but only because of the limited processing power of the current microcomputers. Each of these languages share the ability to make deductions and to handle the multitude of decision that the computer must make.

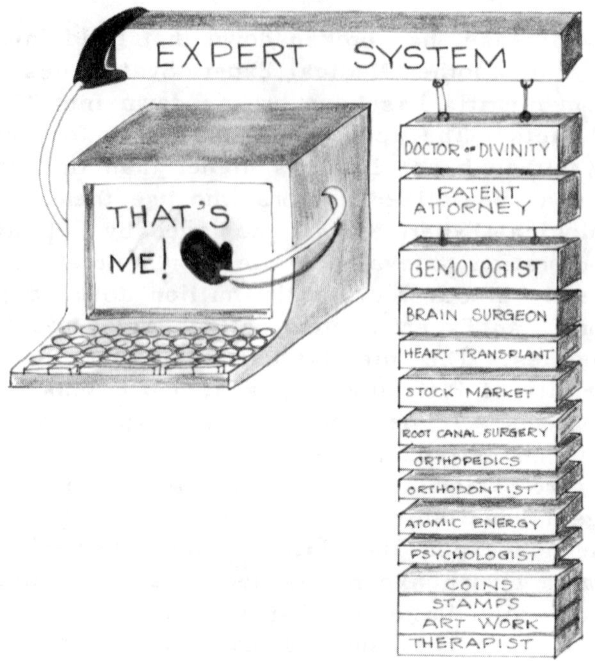

EXPERT SYSTEMS

Figure 4.2.1

Expert Systems raise many ethical questions. Can a Gemology Expert System be credible in the hands of a jeweler? Can a Copyright Law Expert System be trusted in the hands of a paralegal? Can a Medical Expert System be trusted in the hands of a nurse? The answers are not clear, but the human expert will still be needed to question and audit the computer. To know if the advice the computer give is accurate -- not just believable -- will still be the job of the expert in the fields that use the Expert System.

The Japanese

In April, 1982, the Japanese government and computer industry set out on an organized ten year mission -- to develop the Fifth Generation computer. To understand fully what the Fifth Generation is, let us step back for just a moment to look at what the first four were:

Generation One: The Vacuum Tube
Generation Two: The Transistor
Generation Three: The Integrated Circuit
Generation Four: The Very-Large-Scale Integrated Circuit

COMPUTER GENERATIONS

Table 4.2.2

Generation one was what made electronic computers possible, but were too mammoth to be practical for every one. Generation two reduced the size of computers but it was still out of reach for most of us. Generation three brought computers into more and more businesses and universities. And Generation four made possible the widespread use of very powerful computers. The fifth generation will be the intelligent and widespread use of computers using parallel processing (many computers or microprocessors working in tandem to simulate the human mind -- most all computers today use serial processing (one process following the next))to carry out expert-like functions.

We know the Japanese plan to widely distribute super-microcomputers with Expert Systems and they are using Prolog to develop the systems. They are, in turn, developing the microprocessors to handle AI. We know laser disk technology will store the massive amounts of information and that these systems will use natural language interfaces that will enable the user to speak to the computer in plain English. Yet, if we know so much, why aren't we there yet?

There are several reasons. The Fifth Generation will have more powerful Very-Large-Scale Integrated Circuits (VLSI) running in parallel with natural language Artificial Intelligent software. These VLSI circuits are the equivalent of 100,000 and more transistors on a single microprocessor. As these circuits reach into the millions, whole computers and their operating systems will fit onto a single microprocessor. As microprocessors become smaller and more powerful, personal computers will get smaller and more powerful, as well.

To understand how long all of this will take, we need only to look at the current microprocessors under testing and in production. Usually it takes from 3 to 4 years to see a microprocessor model swing into full use. First, the microprocessor must be manufactured in enough quantity to drive the price down; second, machines must be designed to use the microprocessor; third, software must be written to take advantage of the new machine. So, the microprocessors in testing now, will, more than likely, be in full use in 3 to 4 years. For example, Future Computing, Inc., predicted that, by 1988, an IBM PC or its compatible will probably be a 16/32 bit microprocessor machine with at least 2 megabytes of Random Access Memory (RAM), at least 100 megabytes of hard disk storage with a 1/4 inch tape backup, an advance graphics and communications processor, with a built in 2400 baud modem. This machine will be capable of voice recognition and will more than likely have a read-only laser disk with over one-million bytes of applications programs on it. There predictions are probably made based on the current state-of-the-art microprocessors in existence but not yet in full production. The cost for all of this? Probably less than $5,000!

The Japanese are learning at an incredibly fast rate. Even if they do not meet their goal of Artificial Intelligence on personal computers by 1992, by trying, they will be light years ahead of those who aren't also trying.

Because of antitrust laws, American companies have problems in combining their research projects. Will we fall behind the Japanese? Some people firmly believe that those who control knowledge, control power. Fortunately, the Japanese do plan to share this knowledge with others.

Today, the Japanese have not entered the computer market en masse. Until lately, they lacked a standard upon which they could grasp, expand, and overrun as they have in the stereo and TV industries. Like the Romans, the Japanese have come and they have seen, but they have not yet conquered -- they seem to be perching on branches waiting. The standard they may eventually trounce on may be the IBM PC. Already we have seen inroads of Japanese firms such as Fujitsu, Matsushita, Mitsubishi, Sanyo, and Panasonic in America. One problem they have experienced is a lack of strong distribution channels within the United States. To smooth their way, one method used often (since their names do not have product recognition in America as do American companies such as Apple, IBM and DEC) is joint ventures with American firms.

In any event, what should an Expert System be like? To be useful, they must follow certain guidelines. They should be natural and easy for the user. They should be fast, flexible, modular, and modifiable. As rules are added, their accuracy and reliability should increase; alternately when rules are taken away, performance should decrease. Uncertainty is built into the system and the user should be able to ask the Expert System how it came to its answer -- an audit trail. Most importantly, the system should work and be invisible to the user.

Why, in a book about jewelry and computers, spend so much time talking about Artificial Intelligence and the Japanese? If the jeweler has read this far he should know the answer. The pace of the computer evolution is such that we cannot ignore it; we should be aware of it, and attempt to understand it. To do so, we have to see where it has been, where it is, and where it is going. Knowing these facts will prepare you to make smarter decisions about computers. You will know what questions to ask, and will be more familiar with what you want and don't want. Mostly, you will see the computer in perspective and be prepared to meet it on its terms, at its level. And you'll be better off for it.

A word of caution. Those who have used a computer from its beginning (although I am not one of these people) tell us that a computer is a tool: the information that comes from it should be regarded with the same scrutiny given to vegetables, fruit, and meat at the grocery store. Even though we squeeze, smell, and look at it -- we still buy bad food, yet by selecting the right foods we are nourished, and our bodies and minds refreshed. So it is with computers: the data that they present looks convincing, sometimes too convincing -- always question, always double check. But learn, too, that when used as a tool it is an extension of our minds. When you do, you'll have taken the first step beyond the first ring. And, you may find yourself in a world of infinite possibilities . . . in the world of the computer.

APPENDIX A

List by job title hours performed in the below (per week):

Job title________________________ HOURS

Sales presentations to customers ______
Housekeeping and cleaning ______
Store meetings ______
Training(on the job) ______
Windows and displays ______
Appraisals ______
Putting out inventory ______
Advertising ______
Repair and appraisal take in ______
Repair work ______
Bookkeeping

- a. Accounts payable ______
- b. Accounts receivable ______
- c. Payroll ______
- d. Word processing and typing ______
- e. Open-to-buys ______
- f. Financial analysis and budgeting ______
- g. Repair job tracking ______
- h. Inventory control ______
- i. General Ledger ______
- j. Mailing lists ______
- k. File upkeep ______
- l. General record maintenance ______
- m. Receiving stock ______
- n. Transferring stock ______
- o. Shipping stock ______
- p. Layaway tracking ______
- q. Other ______

Management

- a. Financial planning ______
- b. Hiring ______
- c. Memo and reports ______
- d. Follow-up ______
- e. Troubleshooting ______
- f. Training ______
- g. Scheduling ______
- h. Entertaining ______
- i. Lectures and meetings ______
- j. Salesman and buying ______
- k. Work brought home ______
- l. Scheduling ______

TOTAL HOURS ______

BREAKDOWN BY JOB OF HOURS WORKED

Table 1.2.3

Number of employees currently employed?______________
List all employee job titles and hours each works per week:

Titles	Hours per week
______________________	____
______________________	____
______________________	____
______________________	____
______________________	____
______________________	____
______________________	____
______________________	____
______________________	____
______________________	____
	TOTAL HRS____

APPROXIMATE TOTAL HOURS OF ALL EMPLOYEES

Table 1.2.2

Glossary

ALIASING--The step effect created by the low resolution of some computer monitors. The higher the resolution the less stepping is evident.

ALPHA-NUMERIC--Representing both letters and numbers.

AMERICAN STANDARD CODE FOR INFORMATION INTERCHANGE (ASCII)--A set of symbols number from 1 to 128 that account for most of the symbols used on modern typewriters and keyboards.

ARTIFICIAL INTELLIGENCE--The ability of a computer to display functions thought of as connected with human intelligence.

ASSEMBLY LANGUAGE--A language composed of mnemonic symbols that are later converted to machine language.

AUTOMATION--The general practice of applying computers to solve or assist with administrative, sales, accounting, and other general business matters. Automation may be implemented in whole or part through the use of computers in a daily business atmosphere.

AVERAGE COLLECTION PERIOD--The average mumber of days account receivable dollars stay outstanding. This helps analysts to determine the chances of collecting a firm's receivables.

BALANCE FORWARD--A method used in the Accounts Receivable segment of accounting software that brings the balance only forward to the next accounting period. This is in lieu of bringing the details of that account forward (see OPEN ITEM) into the next accounting period.

BAR CODE--Marking products using bars of different thicknesses to represent numbers and characters, such as (UPC) Universal Product Codes, 3 of 9, Codabar, and others.

BAR CODE SCANNER--An optical unit that can display and transfer the information of a bar code to a computer. In the Ideal Jewelry Program bar code scanners will be able to store data for later uploading to a computer.

BATCH FILE--A special command for the computer to perform a series of predefined tasks without operator intervention; when combined with a timer function it will permit the computer to operate without an operator present. The batch file is called a shell script in the UNIX operating system.

BITS--Binary digit-abbreviated. Meaning one of two values ((on-off) (1-0) (yes/no) (high voltage/low voltage)).

BAUD--The number of discrete signaling units per second used in determining the speed at which a computer can transmit information.

BINARY CODE--Or machine language--Code made up of two different values assigned to each code element.

BITS--Binary digit-abbreviated. Meaning one of two values (on-off) (1-0) (yes/no).

BYTE--Means eight bits used as a unit, it can be two numbers or one character. A byte can be regarded as a word made up of the alphabet of bits. The more bytes the machine is capable of moving around within its processor at the same time, the larger is its short term memory and ability to process quickly.

"C" LANGUAGE--A portable and powerful computer language that is used to develop many of todays integrated programs. It was developed by Bell Laboratories.

CASH CONVERSION CYCLE--Represents the time involved in converting a sale into cash on hand. The quicker this cycle is, the better the cash flow posture of the business.

CAT-1--An expert system designed to help non-expert diesel repair people troubleshoot diesel engines.

CODABAR--A code system using special symbols and numbers, it is used by the Library of Congress, on blood bags and photo finishing bags,etc.

CODE 39--An alpha-numeric bar code that can be read in two directions with a bar code scanner and can vary in length. "3 of 9" means each character is nine elements, three of which will be wide.

COMMAND DRIVEN--No menus are offered to the user (although the commands could be used to create menus). The instructions or choices must be known by the user to perform various functions in a program. It offers greater flexibility and control of data.

COMPILER--A low level program that generates a machine language program from a high level language.

COMPUSERVE--An on-line textual data base system that contains data covering a very broad base of topics, ie. diamond prices, commodities and stocks, Special Interest Groups (SIG), and so forth. Compuserve can be accessed through communication software, a modem, and telephone

CONCURRENCY--Another term for multi-tasking, performing more than one job at a time.

CONNECT TIME--The time a person actually spends connected to a telecommunication network or on a time-sharing computer, which is a computer that keeps track of time spent on the system for billing purposes. Time sharing also denotes a multi-user computer system in which all users share the computer for time of the central processor.

COST-OF-OPPORTUNITY--When inventory is not turning over quickly enough, the cost-of-opportunity is the money spent on overhead, employees, and inventory that could have been earning interest in a bank.

CRASH--An unscheduled shutdown of a computer due to problems with the hardware or software.

CUT-AND-PASTE--Process of transferring and integrating data with the use of windows. It can also be called "using a clipboard". It also means moving blocks of text to other areas of text in a word processing file. Writers and editors would usually cut and paste pieces of paper that contained paragraphs and sentences from a written document until it was shaped into the final manuscript or document.

DATA--This term denotes all information (ie. facts, figures, symbols) that can be stored on, used by, and computed with a computer.

DATA BASE--An extensive file of information on a particular topic that is continually updated.

DATA ENTRY--The process of entering data into a computer.

DEBUGGING--The act of finding and removing problems, errors, or malfunctions from software or hardware.

DEPTH--The number of one style of jewelry stocked.

DISKS--Magnetic storage devices that hold or store a program by magnetic pulses. Disks can be floppy, hard, or laser. Each has its own unique characteristics and advantages. The hard disk typically holds millions of bytes of data; the laser disk holds hundreds of millions to billions of bytes of information whereas the floppy --

commonly seen on personal computers -- holds hundreds of thousands of bytes of information (a double spaced type written page is about 2000 bytes of data).

DOWNLOAD--Receiving data from another computer into a target computer via a serial or parallel port. Infers from you to me.

ELECTRONIC MAIL--The replacement of inter and intra office paper correspondence through the use of computers and software specially designed to accommodate the greater throughput potential of electronic data.

EXPERT SYSTEMS--A thinking machine that has both the knowledge and intuition of an expert in a certain field. Heuristics is the study of artificial intelligence. Expert systems require a limited set of rules, a narrow field of knowledge, an audit trail, a means to learn from its mistakes, and a knowledge manager to work effectively with experts while developing the expert system. These programs are generally written in LISP, Prolog, or Forth.

FILE--An accumulation of data on a certain topic or for a certain purpose. These are the equivalent to files in a file cabinet in that each contains information on a specific topic. Files are identified by file names.

FILE SERVER--A computer used in a Local Area Network (LAN) as the mother node. The file server usually contains a hard disk, printer, and other input/output (I/O) devices. It may or may not be able to be used as a stand alone computer while it acts as the network server.

FLOAT--The amount of money in checks written but not yet received by the bank for payment.

HARDWARE--The solid, metal or "hard" component parts of a computer.

HISTORICAL DATA--Past sales records on an item in inventory. Historical data can be reviewed to determine the salability and stocking position of individual items of jewelry.

ICONS--Illustrative images used to instruct the computer to perform a particular task. The icon is similar to verbal menus but lets common symbols take the place of words. This saves space and lets more people understand choices quicker.

INPUT/OUTPUT DEVICE--Device such as a modem, printer, bar code reader, etc. that enables the computer to deal with the outside world.

INTEGRATION--An elusive concept in programming that uses a common command syntax throughout the various modules of a program. Data can be transferred more freely and easier than non-integrated programs. There are varying degrees of integration. Ultimately, the greatest degree of compatibility to other programs while retaining an integrated nature should be the design of an integrated package.

INTERNIST/CADUCES--Expert system that examines 500 diseases and 3500 symptoms.

JULIAN DATE--A four digit code in which the first digit stands for the last digit of the current year, the last three digits stand for the number of days since the first day of the year. An example follows: 6030 or January 30, 1986. In reality this could be any decade but in business uses, most people will be able to relate the julian date with the current decade.

KNOWLEDGE MANAGERS--The developers of expert systems who extract knowledge from a professional and put it into a computer program. The knowledge manager attempts to break a field of knowledge down into a set of closely defined rules and inferences.

LANGUAGE(COMPUTER)--A set of symbols a computer will understand and the rules to control those symbols.

LASER--A coherent beam of light, emitted from a device designed to create light energy at one frequency. LASER stands for Light Amplification by Stimulation of Emission of Radiation.

LASER PRINTER--A printer that uses a laser beam and a complex series of reflectors and refractors that is capable of producing high resolution graphics and text at speeds in excess of 300 characters per second. The quality is significantly better than most other computer printers. Many laser printers use copier technology to produce the final image. Prices of these printers have come down to a level that jewelers can finally afford, but they are still at least twice as expensive as most printers on the market. The print in this book was set by a Corona Laser Printer (Model LP-300).

LEAD TIME--The time it takes to order and receive an item. Different items will have different lead times. These can be determined and this information used to assist the jeweler in placing orders for merchandise.

MACHINE DEPENDENCE--Program that only works on one machine or microprocessor. Program must be rewritten to run on another machine.

MAILMERGE--Capacity of a word processor to use a mailing list data base to create letters containing personalized information. This name is also a trademark of the Compupro Company for their Mailmerge program.

MAINFRAME--Large computers that process quantities of data at rapid speeds with access to billions of characters of data. They are characterized by their multiuser and multi-tasking nature.

MENU-DRIVEN--Offers the user a list of instructions or

messages so that an option may be chosen to perform various functions in a program. This is less flexible and slower than command-driven programs, yet easier to use. This is important in an environment in which many novice computer users need to access the computer.

MICROCOMPUTER--A small computer system consisting basically of a monitor screen, keyboard and limited data storage. It is based upon a microprocessor. It is versatile due to small size, trustworthy performance and low weight, power, and cost.

MICROPROCESSORS--The small single silicon chip on which is contained the electronic components of an entire central processor. It is one of the main parts of a microcomputer. This is the brain of the computer in which all the computations are performed in binary form. A microprocessor can be compared to thousands of tiny on-off switches or gates. These switches perform the logic for which computers are so noted. Most are the size of wafer cookies or smaller.

MINICOMPUTER--A computer system having greater performance capabilities and higher prices than microcomputers, but with less storage, slower processing speeds, and lower cost than a mainframe computer.

MODEM--A modulator-demodulator device that converts digital signals into telephone signals and back again.

MOUSE--A mechanical or optical pointing device used to move the cursor about the computer display. It's name comes from its shape: it is designed to fit the hand comfortably. Some programs and operating systems make special use of the mouse, ie. the Apple "MacIntosh" line of computers.

MULTI-TASKING--More than one program is run on a computer at the same time. One program runs in the foreground and others in background. Some computers, through the use of windows, can run more than one application in the foreground.

MULTI-USER--More than one terminal can be used at the same time to run more than one program.

MYCIN--A medical expert system used by non-specialist doctors to detect and treat meningitis.

NETWORK, LOCAL AREA--The connection of more than one computer for the purpose of sharing peripheral devices (such as printers, modems, hard disks, and so forth) and for distributed sharing of information including common data bases, inter and intra office mail, and telecommunication's information. Networks are usually connected to a file server in one of several topologies.

NO-HIT--Merchandise that has not sold. Being able to identify these items can lead to greater stock turn and sale of these items.

NON-SIM--Classification for an item that sells only once in six months. It stands for Non-Special Inventory Item Management. A SIM item will convert to Non-SIM if after 6 months it is not hit one or more times. The U.S. Navy uses this method in its inventory management programs.

NORTH AMERICAN PRESENTATION LEVEL PROTOCOL SYNTAX (NAPLPS) -- A symbolic system of coding videotext images so that they can be transferred easily and quickly on telecommunication networks, ie. phones and so forth.

ON-LINE--Denotes currently in use or over a telecommunications network, ie. He is on-line with his other store or the on-line data base contains information that I can give you as soon as I have received it.

OPEN ITEM--A method used in the Accounts Receivable portion of some accounting software that keeps the details of an account open from accounting period to accounting period. This differs from the Balance forward method (see BALANCE FORWARD).

OPEN SYSTEM--(see OPEN ITEM).

OPEN-TO-BUYS--A budget established by the jeweler allocating dollars available for inventory based on anticipated sales. It protects the jeweler from overspending dollars on excess inventory during low sale periods.

OPERATING SYSTEM--A low level language program, usually written in assembly language, that carries out the commands of the programs in progress. It acts as the air traffic controller for software and hardware.

PARALLEL PROCESSING--In regard to Artificial Intelligence, refers to a process similar to that of the human brains ability to carry on more than one function at a time through the use of separate processors (separate portions of the brain), ie. walking and talking, breathing and knitting, day-dreaming and driving.

PERSONAL COMPUTER DISK OPERATING SYSTEM (PC DOS version 3.1)--An operating system developed by Microsoft of Bellevue, WA. It is the standard operating system used on the IBM PC line of computers. Version 3.1 is the networking operating system that was mentioned in Part One that has opened the door to using several IBM PC compatible computers in a jewelry store. The advantage to using it is that not only do powerful accounting programs run under it, but that over 6,000 additional programs will run under it, too.

PERIPHERALS--In regard to computers, these are the accessory equipment that gives the computer its various abilities to communicate with the humankind, ie. printers, keyboards, monitors, and so forth. Another term commonly used is Input/Output (I/O) devices.

PERPETUAL INVENTORY--This term is used to describe an inventory system in which the jeweler will know at all times what his on hand balance of any stock item. He will know how many are on order, how many have been received, and how many have been sold.

PIXEL(Picture element)--The smallest point on a computer monitor that can be manipulated by the computer's program.

POINT-OF-SALE(POS)--Electronic means of automating inventory control using a cash register as means of input. The process can be further simplified by the use of bar codes for stock entry information.

PORTABILITY--Ability of a program or operating system to be used in more than one type of computer without major revision. Programs must be written with portability in mind otherwise a program written in a portable language may not be as portable as one might think. "C" language and Modula 2 are examples of portable languages and UNIX is an example of a portable operating system, which was written mostly in the "C" language.

PORTING--Changing over to another computer, ie. Port a program (so that it will run) from this computer brand to an other computer brand. This term is most frequently used in conjunction with adapting software to run on another type of computer. The act of porting usually requires a change in the source code of a program.

PRINT SPOOLING--Allows a file, which is temporarily loaded into RAM, to be printed while performing other functions on the computer.

PROCESSING TIME--The time a computer uses to carry out the computations of a program. A computer generally does not use its processor to process but a fraction of the time. By switching back and forth between programs, a multi-tasking and multi-user computer makes use of this feature to process more than one program at nearly the same time -- to the operator is seems to be at the same time. The more bits the computer has, the quicker the computer, the more users it can have, and the more programs it can have sharing the processor. This is why some systems get bogged down when many operators vie simultaneously for processing time.

PROGRAM--This is the instructions that are saved on disk, loaded into Random Read-Write Memory (RAM) when needed, and run on a microprocessor to carry out the programmers designed function. A program can be very simple or very complex. The program is what makes the machine behave for the user in the manner that he desires. Even the fastest most sophisticated computer is useless unless it also has fast and sophisticated programs written for it.

PROMPT--Being coached or reminded to perform a predefined task. On a computer, one is often prompted to press a key or take certain prescribed steps. A prompt is also a symbol used to signal a user of a pre-defined status or mode.

PROOF VALUES--An error checking feature used in balancing accounts.

PUFF--A medical expert system on pulmonary disease.

QUALIFIED LEADS--A customer, familiar with a business's products who for whatever reason is a likely candidate to buy that product.

QUERY--Search or request for particular information stored in the memory of a computer.

RANGE--Number of different styles of jewelry stocked.

RANDOM(READ-WRITE) ACCESS MEMORY (RAM)--a very fast method of retrieving information at any storage location in the memory. This is the location to where programs are loaded to and the medium in which they operate to carry out their assigned functions (think of it as an electronic warehouse in which data -- electronic on-off signals -- are constantly being shipped, stored, and moved).

RATIO ANALYSIS--Technique used to compare business profits with overhead costs to get an accurate picture of a business' health. Ration analysis, for the most part, is performed through simple mathematical analysis of key accounting data. A profit and loss statement provides much useful information for Ratio Analysis.

SCANNER--A portable unit used to identify and hold coded information that can later by transferred to a computer such as in a bar code scanner.

SERIAL PORT--An input/output (I/O) device through which the computer talks with printers, modems, mice, and other I/O devices.

SINGLE-TASKING--One program at time can be run on the computer.

SINGLE-USER--Only one person can use a computer at the same time.

SOFTWARE--The languages, programs, and processes of a computer system.

SOURCE CODE--A program written in its original computer language available to other programmers for modification and compilation.

SPECIAL INTEREST GROUP (SIG)--In a computer club or on an on-line data base such as Compuserve or the Source, it is a group of people who are interested in one computer related topic and who meet (in person or on-line) to share information about this topic. In a computer club, an example would be the new member SIG; on Compuserve, a SIG would be all IBM Personal Computer users.

SPECIAL INVENTORY MANAGEMENT(SIM)--Classification for merchandise that sells rapidly-twice in six months. It stands for Selected Item Management. This designation is used by the U.S. Navy in its inventory management systems. By designating jewelry as SIM and Non-SIM allows jewelers to more closely control hot selling items. A SIM program is nothing more than determining what sells and watching these on a routine basis.

SPIFF-Bonus paid to a salesperson for selling a particular piece of jewelry. Often used to create interest in selling slow-moving items.

STOCK TURN--Term used to indicate the amount of times that merchandise sells in a given period of time. One popular formula is

$$\frac{\text{sales at cost}}{\text{average inventory at cost}}$$

SUPERMICROCOMPUTER--The melding of the microcomputer with the minicomputer in a low cost, high power unit, containing many of the features of the both, and usually at a lower cost than a minicomputer (it could also be called a very powerful microcomputer).

TELECOMMUNICATE--A means of transferring data through electrical means, ie. telephone and radio. Computers are capable of transfering vast quantities of information through telecommunications.

TEMPLATE--A mathematical model of a business that uses a spreadsheet program as the basis of its creation.

TERMS CODE--Predefined series of codes representing various terms of credit sales, and so forth.

TOPVIEW--An IBM software program that enables the IBM series of Personal Computers to run software in a manner that makes the sharing of data and commands between programs more of a reality than myth. Other programs have entered the market place but have failed to capture the hearts and minds of the majority of IBM PC users. TOPVIEW gives the IBM PC and AT a multi-tasking capability.

TURNKEY SYSTEM--Situation in which a computer vendor supplies everything needed in one package-hardware and software. The vendor would insure correct operation, installation, and service of the computer and its software. Turnkey systems generally meet a very specific need of the customer and perform that job quite well. Most turnkey systems involve minicomputer systems but, of late, many developers are creating turnkey systems for microcomputers.

TUTORIAL--A help file associated with a computer program that can usually be called upon for assistance or used to teach the operator about functions or feature of the program in use.

UNIVAC--The first commercially available computer developed by Remington Rand in 1951.

UNIX--An operating system developed by AT&T that is multi-user and multi-tasking and is portable from computer to computer. It consists of over 200 utility programs that can be combined in such a synergistic manner that often precludes the need for other more specialized programs.

UPLOAD--Sending data to another computer. Infers from me to you.

UPWARD COMPATIBILITY--A concept started with the IBM/360 operating system and culminated in the UNIX operating system that permits programs to be moved from a computer to its offspring without major revamping.

USER-FRIENDLINESS--A term describing the ease that a novice computer user will experience in learning about a computer or program.

VALIDITY--The degree of accuracy found in inventory records when compared to the actual on-hand count of merchandise. As time passes between storewide (wall-to-wall) inventories the validity of stock records decrease. To restore inventory to a higher validity an inventory either partial or full, should be taken.

VERTICAL SOFTWARE--Programs written for one industry -- each containing features useful to that particular business or industry.

VIDEOTEXT--Term describing the systems used to provide services such as homebanking, shopping, business information, news, weather, and so forth, to homes and businesses. The systems use either telephone connections (viewdata) or unused television broadcast signals. Videotext also is used by many as a replacement word for Viewdata.

VIEWDATA--Offers services similar to videotext, but uses a telephone connection instead of broadcast signals. The viewer can send and receive information via a remote control hand-held keypad.

WAND--Pen-like device used to transfer bar code information to a bar code scanner.

WHAT-IF--An analysis of financial data using an electronic spreadsheet. The analysis is sped up owing to the ability of the computer and the spreadsheet program to quickly change key figures and numbers that permits the fast recalculation of results.

WINDOWS--Portions of memory data displayed in overlapping sections on a screen at one time. These can be different programs or different parts of the same program. It facilitates the user in dealing with a multi-tasking environment. Most windowing programs attempt to integrate the transfer of data from one program to the other. The common input/output (i/o) device used in windowing is the mouse.

WINDOWS (MICROSOFT'S)--A program that integrates many disimilar programs with each other by providing a common command interface. It is similar to TOPVIEW (see TOPVIEW)

WORD PROCESSING--Tasks such as letter writing, printing, editing, and creating mailing lists carried out from a desktop terminal.

WORD PROCESSING SOFTWARE--The programs available that are geared specifically to word processing applications.

WORD PROCESSOR--The desktop unit consisting of a display screen, keyboard and printer that uses software programs to perform word processing tasks.

Index

COLOPHON

This book was written on an IBM PC with 256k memory, two 360k DSDD floppy disk drives. The word processor was PC-Write (Freeware) version 2.0. The type in this book was set using a Corona LP-300 laser printer and the above word processor and computer.

Production data:

Typestyle:

Bookman 9 point proportional for text.
Bookman 12 point proportional for sub-headings.
Bookman 18 point for chapter titles.
Gothic 9 point bold for tables.

Cover Design:

Betty Peterson

Binding:

Perfect (adhesive)

Edition:

First: 2,500

Printing:

Offset, BookCrafters, Chelsea, MI

COMPUTER
DEVELOPMENTS

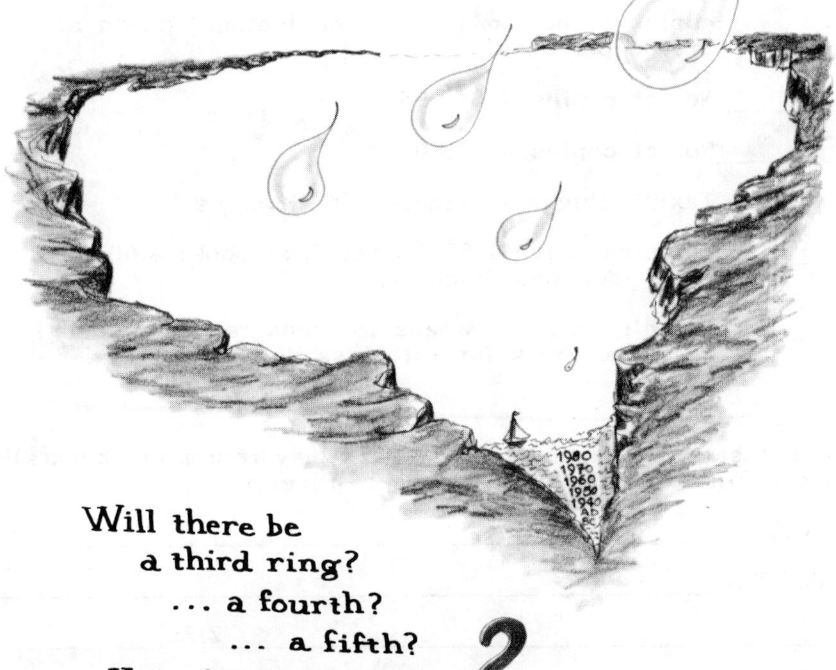
1980
1970
1960
1950
1940
AD
BC
Will there be
a third ring?
... a fourth?
... a fifth?
How far can it go ...?

ORDER FORM

Pimiteoui Publications
P.O. Box 48-1
Rodney, MI 49432-0048

Please send me the following quantity of "The Second Ring: A Jeweler's Guide to Computers":

_____copies (perfect bound) at $19.95 each.

_____copies of custom hand-bound leather edition at $75.00 per book.

_________No. of copies X $19.95.

_________No. of copies X $75.00.

_________Tax: Michigan residents add 4% sales tax.

_________Shipping: Add $1.50 for the first book; $.50 for each additional book or,

_________I can't wait 3-4 weeks for book rate. Included is $2.75 per book for 1st class delivery.

_________Total.

If not satisfied, I understand that I may return the book(s) for a full refund within 30 days of receipt.

NAME:____

ADDRESS:____

______________________________________ZIP:____________

Payment method: ____ Master Card ____ Visa

____ Check ____ Money order

Card number:______________________________

Date Expires:_____________________________

Cardholder's
Signature:________________________________

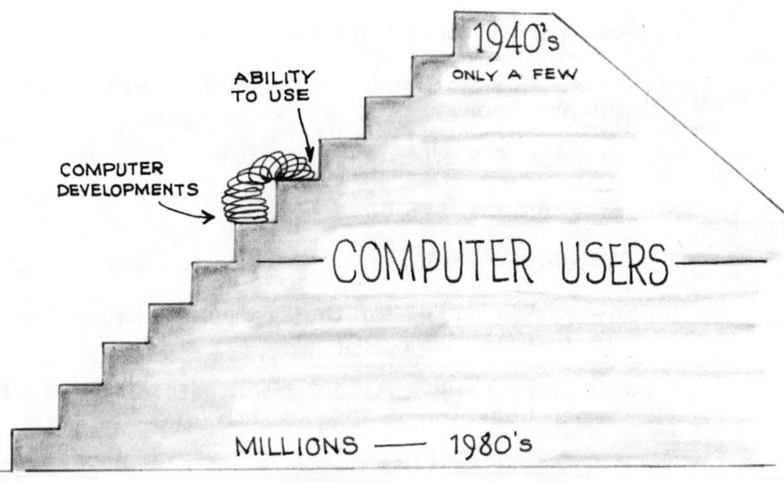

SLINKY EFFECT

Is it bottomless?

Constant computer developments, with increased ability to use them staying close behind, create a continuous somersaulting effect.

ORDER FORM

Pimiteoui Publications
P.O. Box 48-1
Rodney, MI 49432-0048

Please send me the following quantity of "The Second Ring: A Jeweler's Guide to Computers":

_____copies (perfect bound) at $19.95 each.

_____copies of custom hand-bound leather edition at $75.00 per book.

________No. of copies X $19.95.

________No. of copies X $75.00.

________Tax: Michigan residents add 4% sales tax.

________Shipping: Add $1.50 for the first book; $.50 for each additional book or,

________I can't wait 3-4 weeks for book rate. Included is $2.75 per book for 1st class delivery.

________Total.

If not satisfied, I understand that I may return the book(s) for a full refund within 30 days of receipt.

NAME:____

ADDRESS:____

____ZIP:____________

Payment method: ____ Master Card ____ Visa

____ Check ____ Money order

Card number:_____________________________

Date Expires:_____________________________

Cardholder's
Signature:_______________________________